COGNITIVE PLANNING

COGNITIVE PLANNING

THE PSYCHOLOGICAL BASIS OF INTELLIGENT BEHAVIOR

J. P. Das

Binod C. Kar

Rauno K. Parrila

Sage Publications

New Delhi/Thousand Oaks/London

First published in 1996 by

Sage Publications India Pvt Ltd
M-32, Greater Kailash Market I
New Delhi 110 048

Sage Publications Inc
2455 Teller Road
Thousand Oaks, California 91320

Sage Publications Ltd
6 Bonhill Street
London EC2A 4PU

Published by Tejeshwar Singh for Sage Publications India Pvt Ltd, typeset by Par Graphics, New Delhi, and printed at Baba Barkhanath Printers, Delhi.

Library of Congress Cataloging-in-Publication Data

Das J. P. (Jagannath Prasad)
    Cognitive planning: the psychological basis of intelligent behavior/J. P. Das, Binod C. Kar, Rauno K. Parrila.
        p. cm.
    Includes bibliographical references and index.
    1. Planning–Psychological aspects. 2. Human information processing. 3. Cognitive psychology. I. Kar, Binod C., 1942- . II. Parrila, Rauno K., 1961–   III. Title.
BF433. P6D37   1996   153.4–dc20   96–12246

ISBN: 0–8039–9287–4 (US)   81–7036–522–8 (India)

Sage Production Editor: Indiver Nagpal

To
our parents
and J. P.'s grand-daughters
Silpi and Soumya

CONTENTS

LIST OF TABLES AND FIGURES

ACKNOWLEDGMENTS

This monograph on planning is a joint effort of three writers. It incorporates the research done in four different countries including Canada, Finland, India, and the United States of America. We are therefore indebted to people in places where the research was carried out and to the institutions that supported it. Among those people are: Drs Seija Äystö (Finland), Udaya Dash (India), Purnima Mathur (India), Amulya Khurana (India), Sasi Misra (India), Rama Mishra (Canada), and Jack A. Naglieri (United States), and their students. Institutions include the Universities of Alberta, Jyväskylä, Ohio State, and Utkal, the Indian Institute of Management, Ahmedabad, and the Indian Institute of Technology, Delhi. Secretarial and research assistance received in each of these institutions are gratefully acknowledged. Finally, special appreciation for editorial work done goes to Serge Hein, graduate student at the University of Alberta.

INTRODUCTION

This book is divided into two major parts. The first part, consisting of Chapters 1 to 4, reviews existing planning literature from historical, cognitive, neuropsychological, and developmental perspectives, and also explains the theoretical orientation of the book. The second part consists of Chapters 5 and 6. In it we describe several empirical studies that we have undertaken in order to understand the operation of planning in different situations.

We open the book with a theoretical review of planning within the context of cognitive psychology, which is the central theme of Chapter 1. Cognitive psychology is frequently described as a reaction to the behavioristic psychology associated with Watson. In actuality, however, it existed before behavioristic psychology became prominent and only reassumed its importance in the 1960s when the study of behavior lost its preeminence.

Prior to behaviorism, several individuals, most notably William James in 1890 and Sir Fredrick Bartlett in 1932, were concerned with cognitive topics such as attention and reconstructed memory. Even during the peak of behaviorism, Tolman and Hull displayed traces of cognitivism in their explanations of animal behavior. Cognitive psychology was also sustained throughout this period and even prior to it by its applications to the psychology of language. The unique role of language as a cognitive tool was elaborated upon earlier in this century in Pavlov's (1942) second signalling system and Vygotsky's studies in the late 1920s on thought and language. The same position has been taken by contemporary theorists such as Donald (1993). Donald regarded the evolution of language as the distinguishing element between human beings and other primates. He also united the study of cognition with the study of the evolution of the brain. In Chapter 1, the concern with the study of the brain is linked to the social constructive nature of the evolution of the brain and to the formative influence of culture on cognitive processes.

Next, the "cognitive revolution" is traced briefly up to the emergence of information theory and the development of computer sciences. These two perspectives converged in artificial intelligence research and the development of different problem-solving machines and programs.

The progression from problem solving to planning was a simple one and the book by Miller, Galanter, and Pribram (1960) on the nature of plans and the structure of behavior became a benchmark for cognitive psychologists. The ideas presented in their book and the subsequent research that it inspired are reviewed in some detail. A consideration of planning from a neuropsychological perspective (e.g., Luria, 1966) is also presented in order to avoid an overly mechanistic account of planning. Sperry's (1993) call for a "top-down" view of mental functions as determined by environmental and cultural influences further reminds us that planning is a complex cognitive function that is perhaps unique to human beings and that cannot be described adequately by either programming languages or cell biology.

Finally, at the end of Chapter 1, planning is discussed in comparison to closely related notions such as problem solving, strategies, and metacognition. The main focus here is on the isolation of components common to planning and problem solving. Planning is presented as a more pervasive and general regulating process than problem solving. Planning is also distinguished from strategies, with plans being more general and at a "higher" level of analysis. Furthermore, metacognition is a term that is frequently used in association with planning, although there still is a lack of consensus regarding its definition. Metacognition, or knowledge about what one knows, is useful during learning and instruction but again, we believe that planning is a broader concept. In addition to awareness of what an individual knows, planning involves both the allocation of attentional resources and the regulation of cognitive processes.

In Chapter 2 we provide a framework, the PASS theory, within which planning can be conceptualized. After providing a simplified description of the brain's anatomy, we describe the functional organization of the brain. The four cognitive processes are organized around the functions of the occipital–parietal region (simultaneous processing), the fronto–temporal region (successive processing), the frontal region including the prefrontal region (planning), and the brain-stem with its extensive connections to the frontal lobes (arousal–attention). Planning processes are closely connected with the posterior portion of the brain as well as with those regions whose major function is arousal–attention. Knowledge base is recognized as essential to all four cognitive processes. It obviously consists of the products of culture, language, and other symbolic systems, which are the "cognitive tools" (Vygotsky, 1986). The role of these cognitive tools is considered as we define planning as an intrapsychological process that uses symbol systems such as language. This definition is then expanded by discussing the three levels of analysis suggested by Leontjev (1978)—activity, action, and operation—and how they relate to planning.

In order to operationalize planning in terms of tests, we need not only a theory but also a thorough grounding in cognitive psychology and neuropsychology. In the first·chapter, we discuss the cognitive psychological background of planning and in Chapter 3 we discuss the neuropsychological background for understanding planning. The frontal lobes are essential for planning but these alone cannot sustain the complex activities involved in planning. Bearing this in mind, the organization of the planning function is discussed in relation to the three other functional units in the PASS model. The frontal lobes perform an integrative and regulatory function and the different parts are associated with specific functions such as drive, sequencing, motivation, and will. The prefrontal cortex is associated with perhaps the most important function: consciousness. The complex functions of planning and consciousness (i.e., self-awareness or self-reflection) can be disentangled, identified, and studied by observing neurologically impaired patients. The implications of frontal lobe lesions for patient behavior are therefore discussed in this chapter. Much informative data can be obtained by observing the problem-solving behavior of neurological patients: What types of problems they can solve? How does the patient proceed to solve them? Such information can also be useful in tracing the development of planning functions in childhood.

A comprehensive account of the development of planning is given in Chapter 4. The development of planning is discussed in two major fields: (*a*) developmental psychology, following Piaget and Vygotsky, and (*b*) developmental neuropsychology, which relates the development of the brain to cognitive development. Both approaches are integrated, however, in tracing the development of planning during infancy and early and later childhood. The question of what develops with planning is also answered. Plans become more flexible, yet work within the given constraints of the problem, and information is organized within higher conceptual units. Adults and peers contribute to children's development of planning as do their school experiences. Finally, the role of speech and language is discussed from a Vygotskian perspective. Again, we remind ourselves that a connection between the different stages of planning development and the various functions of the brain exists and remains to be researched further.

The second part of the book can best be described as a series of explorations into planning using a few selected planning tasks—explorations that revealed to us the vast range of topics that can be investigated using the tasks as instruments and how important the task parameters are in determining the results of the studies. The instrument used in the studies reviewed in Chapter 5 is Visual Search, a perceptual planning task that straddles the line dividing attention and planning. The task enabled us to explore both automatic search, which requires little cognitive effort, and its contrast, controlled search, in which attention must be allocated and strategies used. Automatic search is parallel, whereas controlled search is serial. The tasks used in our studies were given in paper-and-pencil form rather than in computer form but surprisingly we were able to reproduce the results of the computer form of the task.

Some of the results from our visual search experiments were as follows. Automatic search in which the target of the search belonged to a different category than the distractors (e.g., searching for a picture among numbers) was faster than controlled search (e.g., searching for a number target among other numbers). When the number of distractors was increased, controlled search time increased but automatic search time did not. There were also some unexpected findings. For example, in the automatic search condition, when the target was a picture in a field of numbers, the search time was lower than when the target was a number in a field of pictures. We explained this discrepancy by assuming that when the distractors were pictures, there was enough dissimilarity between them to slow down the search. In contrast, when the distractors were single numbers, the dissimilarity between them was vastly reduced. In other words, numbers were more familiar to the subjects. Search is faster when we can gloss over the distractors and quickly identify the clearly distinct target. Do individuals encode each and every distractor item? It would seem that they do not. In fact, from another experiment, it appears that subjects who were able to name the distractor items more quickly displayed no advantage in search time. The critical element here appears to be the speed with which distractor items can be filtered out and fast filtering does not seem to require naming them.

A greater familiarity with numbers can be assumed for schooled children than for unschooled children. The question, then, is: Will the schooled group exhibit faster automatic search when the distractors are numbers and the target is a picture? In a study that we report in Chapter 5, the schooled group did, in fact, exhibit faster search. In this way, we have explored several aspects of search behavior and delineated both the parameters of the task and the characteristics of individuals that affect search time. We hope that the knowledge gained through the use of this simple task can be used specifically to study the derangements in planning displayed by neurologically impaired patients.

In Chapter 6 we report on studies that utilized various versions of two conceptual planning tasks, Planned Composition and Crack-the-Code. Individual differences in both Planned Composition and Crack-the-Code scores have been found to be related to individual differences in visual search performance. Thus, all three belong to the category of planning tasks.

This chapter consists of three sections. The first section explores the role of speed and working memory in performing Crack-the-Code. A substantial finding is that speed is not as important as working memory for successful Crack-the-Code performance. Thus, in old age or in other conditions that retard performance, Crack-the-Code performance should not be impaired but if working memory is weakened, performance should be poor. Crack-the-Code is therefore a valuable test for separating the influence of speed and working memory on problem solving.

The second section of Chapter 6 concentrates on planning in narrative writing and managerial decision making. Both Planned Composition and Crack-the-Code tasks are used to explore competence in writing narratives and expository text. With regard to narrative writing, we found that performance on other planning tasks could predict writing competence for children who were at least reasonably good writers but it could not predict writing competence for children who were poor writers. The latter group was still struggling to acquire the mechanics of writing.

In the two other studies, all subjects were reasonably good writers: They were university students, some of whom were in management programs. In the first study, subjects were required to write an essay justifying their solution to a management problem. The goal of the study was to refine a rating scale for essays that assesses originality and organization in writing, as well as the writing skills. In the second study, subjects' essay rating scale scores were compared to their competence in Crack-the-Code. A positive correlation was found between these two measures, thereby opening the possibility of using Crack-the-Code performance as a predictor of decision-making competence.

In a subsequent study we therefore report on an attempt to identify individuals whose job performance is rated as either good or poor and to then explore whether members of these two groups can be distinguished on the basis of their Crack-the-Code performance. This was found to be the case: Subjects whose job performance was rated as good by their supervisors scored higher on Crack-the-Code than subjects whose job performance was rated as poor. Thus, we have begun to expand the utility of planning tests into the field of management.

Finally, the third section of Chapter 6 examines the use of verbal protocols for monitoring strategies during problem solving. In the last exploratory study discussed, the usefulness of collecting verbal protocols for delineating the strategies used by younger and older children completing Crack-the-Code was demonstrated. More complex strategies were used by older children and among children of the same age, a variety of strategies was evident. Moreover, a large portion of this variability could not be detected with more traditional product measures, suggesting that analyzing verbal protocols can substantially increase our knowledge about the development of planning.

In the final chapter, we present some possibilities for future research. We select an idea from each of the theoretical chapters and design a study based upon that idea. Planning is a uniquely human characteristic and a higher order cognitive activity that is influenced by cultural learning. We express the hope that both the reviews and the experiments presented in this book will be useful for designing more studies that will help us to better understand this intriguing and complex cognitive function.

1

Planning and the Cognitive Paradigm

Content and Issues: From Past to Present

During recent years, psychologists have emphasized the role of central mediating mechanisms, strategic variables, and executive or control processes in human cognitive activity. These ideas were largely ignored during the first half of this century because of Watson's call to discard the concept of consciousness and because of the pervasive later influence of behavioristic psychology (Sperry, 1993). In this section, we will retrace the path of cognitive psychology from its early beginnings to its partial eclipse and subsequent growth as a prelude to the consideration of planning, the central theme of this book.

The Regulation of Behavior and the Evolution of Cognition

The quality of mental processes that allows us to selectively attend to various tasks was highlighted by James in his treatment of the conscious and deliberate control of attention. Bartlett (1932, 1958) postulated "schemata" to explain remembering and thinking as constructive processes. Selective utilization of past experiences depends on the individual's "ability to turn round upon its own 'schemata' and to construct them afresh" (Bartlett, 1932, p. 206). Since then, the question has been asked: "Who does the search, selects the strategy and tries?" (Neisser, 1967). Who, in fact, is in control? Who implements action?

The response to these questions has been to equip the organism with control or regulatory processes. Regulatory processes are necessary for purposeful behavior. Purpose is the central determinant of behavior in both rats and humans. Tolman (1948), a purposive behaviorist, observed anticipation, goal-directed behavior, and even the use of "cognitive maps" in rats. This was a definite attempt to bridge the gap between stimulus and response with an inner entity: "cognition". The bridge, however, was incomplete. Tolman conceived of a bridge from stimulus to knowledge but he did not explore the path between knowledge and action. Guthrie (1935) expressed this shortcoming as follows:

> In his concern with what goes on in the rat's mind, Tolman has neglected to predict what the rat will do. So far as the theory is concerned the rat is left buried in thought; if he gets to the food-box at the end that is his concern, not the concern of the theory (p. 172).

Other cognitive theorists were no more successful. Köhler (1959, 1927), for example, made the same error when he attempted to explain chimpanzees' "intelligent" behavior using the concept of "insight". Köhler defined insight as "the appearance of a complete solution with reference to the whole lay-out of the [problem] field" (pp. 169-170) and assumed that once the animal has grasped the whole layout (i.e., has gained insight into the problem), the appropriate behavior will follow automatically. But the bridge from knowledge to action was still lacking and the question remained: How are actions controlled by internal representations or, in other words, cognition? The answer is that action is controlled through the mediation of a symbolic system, the best example of which is the use of language as both external and internal speech (Vygotsky, 1978). For the time being, though, let us present a broad view of the evolution of human cognition.

That there is another reality aside from physical, biological, and psychological reality is apparent in Sperry's (1993) article. This "dean of neuroscience" is compelled to consider the cultural world—population pressure, environmental protection, and social order—in order to explain mental functions. Like Pavlov (1928, 1942) before him, he has faith that scientific research has the power to take human society to new heights. He is concerned with the question: How do human beings behave? In other words: How does the mind work to influence behavior?

The representation of knowledge in memory, however, could be too narrow a view of the task of cognitive psychology. Alternatively, the evolution of consciousness as the central point of inquiry in cognitive science may be too broad a view. In terms of knowledge representation, it is already a characteristic human problem because of its dependence on language or some other symbolic system. Donald (1993) suggests that the development of language is what separates human beings from apes and other lower primates. He adds that in the evolution of language, the first step involves the ability to mimic. Many animals exhibit conditioned responses or habitual action patterns (for example, the horse, clever Hans) but they are unable to mimic. In contrast, a newborn infant can mimic four types of facial and mouth expressions within hours of birth. According to Donald, mimicking is succeeded by pointing and rudimentary speech, actions that are willed or deliberately generated by human beings. Both are representational rather than conditional habits, as is evidenced from observing a human infant develop.

LANGUAGE, THOUGHT, AND ACTION: ASSOCIATIONS AND DISSOCIATIONS

The next step involves the full development of language and thinking. Vygotsky (1962) observed that the two have separate origins and do not converge as "verbal thinking" until later in ontogenesis. In its early stages, speech may not always reflect the thoughts of the speaker; in turn, the many complex thoughts of a two-year-old are not translated into speech. But even after speech and thinking initially converge, they do not necessarily overlap in all instances: Not all thinking is verbal and not all speech is intelligible.

One of the central functions of language is that it frees us to refer to objects without the need to manipulate them physically; linguistic representations of knowledge thereby bring about an explosion of interconnected information. Some philosophers have been so impressed by the power of language to construct reality that they have found no need to separate reality and its semantic representation. Language represents all three "mental" functions identified by Greek philosophers—thinking, feeling, and willing (i.e., cognition, affection, and conation, respectively). There are dissociations between language and the three mental activities, however, that are all too apparent. Even as an adult, it is difficult to express one's thoughts accurately! There is, for example, the well-known gap between the intention or will to communicate something and subsequent verbal activity. Similarly, emotions and feelings are not always adequately represented in language. That is, if we cannot express in words everything that we perceive, we certainly cannot express adequately what we feel. Speaking figuratively, there appears to be no direct connection between the eye that perceives or the heart that feels, and the mouth that speaks. Perhaps part of the blame for these difficulties can be placed on an inadequate hardware, namely, the brain.

The Brain and the Social Construction of Behavior

The brain is currently being studied intensively and the neurological properties of mental functions are being scrutinized at different levels. Single neuron analogues of simple learning, such as conditioning, flourished even 30 years ago. But single-cell recordings were insufficient to explain such meaningful activity as learning in which millions of neurons participate. Since then, artificial neural networks have been developed that explain the functioning of the brain at a more inclusive level (Bridgeman, 1993). Long-term potentiation as an important mechanism in explaining learning and memory is also of recent origin (Kandel & Schwartz, 1985). Also, the discovery of new receptors for specific neurotransmitters occurs frequently. At a more molar level, new areas of visual cortex are frequently being discovered for specific visual functions—perhaps at the rate of one each year—and our knowledge of the cortical organization of various memory functions increases even more quickly (see, for example, Squire, Knowlton, & Musen, 1993). It is clear that the psychology of information processing cannot progress in isolation from neurology and molecular biology.

The brain is not a "masterful, unified work of God, but . . . a multifaceted contraption pieced together through evolution, using whatever was at hand to solve problems" (Bridgeman, 1993). Its evolution records many impacts of the sociocultural environments in which human beings not only adapted themselves to live but also created. This leads us to consider the more molar level of evolution, namely, that of cultural evolution.

The social-constructivist position views the evolution of all higher order mental functions as emerging from culture (Vygotsky, 1986). Language provides a convincing example of the cultural evolution of the mind, as well as of the brain. Again, human beings have an advantage. For whatever evolutionary reason, the localization of language in the brain is asymmetrical: The left hemisphere has specialized to take care of complex linguistic functions. This, in turn, means that the right hemisphere had space for developing other functions that may have played an important role in the evolution of the human species. Also, the connection between complex activity and speech is being reexamined through evolutionary evidence. Consider, for example, the possibility that the Broca's area—traditionally regarded as the "speech center" of the brain—developed in two different ways in apes and men, as Greenfield (1991) proposes. She suggests that complex activities, as evidenced in apes (for example, use of tools) are likely controlled by Broca's area. This is in accord with Luria (1973a), who suggested the evolution of speech from activity. The executive functions of speech are located in Broca's area and even the comprehension of verbs (rather than nouns) occurs in the frontal lobe region, close to Broca's area, as revealed by PET scan (Greenfield, 1991).

Thus, cultural evolution has probably accelerated the development of brain systems required to support the emergence of cognitive and noncognitive functions. It is pointed out that when society lacked a widespread mechanism for disseminating knowledge through books, oracy flourished and texts were remembered by bards and *pandits*. In our age of progressive use of visual modes and information storage devices, it is hard to imagine that the brain would not be under pressure to develop new structures (Donald, 1993). Not only the content of thought and its cortical organization but also its structure is determined by the individual's culture, as Luria concluded 60 years ago from his studies of illiterate peoples (Luria, 1973b). In sum, cultural evolution undoubtedly has a pervasive influence on cognition; an influence that is mediated by the tools of cognition as well as cognition's architectural basis in the brain.

THE NATURE OF INTELLIGENCE: THE WEST AND THE EAST

A knotty problem, involving the nature of what is usually referred to as "intelligence", still remains to be considered. Let us regard consciousness, or self-awareness, as the highest cognitive function that is typically human. Knowing about knowing is a frequent pastime of metacognitive knowledge seekers! The content of consciousness varies. But if we can think of a hierarchy of contents, the highest knowledge we must seek to represent in consciousness is, according to an Eastern point of view, *discriminating intelligence*: intelligence that is abstracted from sensory information and from the mechanisms of reasoning and inference for the purpose of discriminating between what is real and what is unreal (Zimmer, 1951).

There are two views of the evolution of consciousness representing true knowledge: a top-down view and a bottom-up view (Das, 1994). Let us begin with a question: Why do the lower primates lack language, that is, a versatile system of decontextualized symbols of representation? According to a bottom-up view, this is due to a lack of vocal equipment for speech and language. Parrots, however, have a superior vocal apparatus compared to apes but cannot be regarded as more intelligent than dolphins and gorillas, for example, who have a possible mental age equivalent to that of a two-year-old human infant.

What does the bottom-up explanation suggest in terms of a symbolic system to represent experience and direct behavior? In humans, the internal stage of evolution, from sensory experience to consciousness representing discriminating intelligence, can be conceived of within a bottom-up framework. The material world contains the five elements of earth, water, light, air, and ether (i.e., space). In order to sense these, the five sensory organs for touch, taste, vision, smell, and hearing (as well as the associated brain areas) developed through the process of natural selection. Apart from the external organs, the internal organs evolved, which gave us our ability to reason, our motivation, and our sense of self. Information originating from these external and internal organs is to be integrated in order to separate the true from the untrue and thus consciousness with discriminating intelligence as its main characteristic must be evolved.

The top-down version is, of course, the reverse. Language evolved because of higher intelligence comprising mental functions such as reasoning, motivation, and the sense of self. The mental functions enable us to represent and integrate sensory experience and thinking. As long as primates lack this higher form of intelligence that culminates in consciousness, language would have no purpose and would not be a basis for evolution. Choosing between the top-down and the bottom-up view presents a knotty problem but note that there is really no mind–body dualism in either version of the evolution of intelligence.

The Information-Processing Approach and the Search for a Mediating Mechanism

The arrival of information theory (see, for example, Broadbent, 1958; Garner, 1956; Shannon, 1948) and its use of terms like input, noise, channel capacity, and output to describe the internal characteristics of the communication system, opened the way for treating cognition as a proper subject matter for scientific study. But information theory was limited because it could not explain adequately the complex, versatile, and active information processing that takes place within the human mind. Humans can increase their information-processing capacity, alter input, store it, reorganize it, retrieve new material beyond the information given, make decisions, and translate these decisions into action (Bruner, Goodnow, & Austin, 1956; Lachman, Lachman, & Butterfield, 1979). It was therefore necessary to specify cognition, the *mediating mechanism*, in more detail in order to explain how all of these activities could possibly occur.

At approximately the same time that information theory was becoming more well known, exciting developments were occurring in the area of computer science. Mathematicians and computer engineers were making tremendous progress in building more powerful computers and creating computer programs that could play chess, prove theorems in logic, and solve calculus problems. These solutions to well-defined and limited problems were interesting and important in stimulating artificial intelligence research. But from the psychologist's point of view, they had one major drawback: Instead of imitating human problem-solving processes they were more or less trying to replace or defeat their human counterparts.

Newell, Shaw, and Simon (1958a, 1958b, 1959) took the next important step forward by developing programs that attempted to simulate human problem-solving processes in logic, trigonometry, and chess. Following their work, more and more cognitive psychologists began to view the human being as a symbol-manipulating information-processing system that takes in symbolic input and then processes it further. These developments formed the basis of what is today known as the information-processing approach in psychology. Miller, Galanter, and Pribram (1960), who are still perhaps the most influential theorists in the area of planning, argued in their seminal book *Plans and the Structure of Behavior* that these new ideas were compatible with, and provided an extension of, established psychological principles. For them, a plan was the connecting link between human information processing and computer programs, as well as the missing connection between knowledge and action.

For cognitive psychologists it was the realization of a dream: "What so many had so long described was finally coming to pass. It is impressive to see, and to experience, the increase in confidence that comes from the concrete actualization of an abstract idea— the kind of confidence a reflex theorist must have felt in the 1930s when he saw a machine that could be conditioned like a dog" (Miller et al., 1960, p. 56). But before we introduce the ideas of Miller et al. about planning in more detail, it is necessary to take a look at the pioneers, Newell, Shaw, and Simon, and to review what they had to say about human problem solving.

PLANNING AS A PROBLEM-SOLVING HEURISTIC

Newell et al. (1958a, 1958b, 1959) assumed that intelligent activity is performed by machines and people alike with the help of (*a*) symbol patterns that represent critical features of the specific problem domain, (*b*) operations on these representations to generate possible solutions, and (*c*) searching through these possibilities to select a solution (multiple solutions are not pursued simultaneously). The simplest form of search, referred to as exhaustive search, involves going through all of the possible alternatives. When the number of possible alternatives is large, however, exhaustive search becomes impractical and often impossible. Most often, human beings solve problems on the basis of judgements that guide search to the most relevant and promising aspects of the problem space. This is referred to as heuristic search.

Newell et al. (1959; see also Newell & Simon, 1972) suggested two ubiquitous and powerful heuristic methods: (*a*) means-end analysis and (*b*) the planning method. Means-end analysis consists of dividing a problem into a sequence of subproblems that are then solved. That is, given the goal and the situation, the difference between the two is defined and a relevant operator is retrieved from the knowledge base in order to reduce the difference. If necessary, this is done one subproblem at a time.

The planning method, in turn, allows the problem solver to construct a solution in general terms before working out the details. It is used when the problem solver (*a*) forms an abstract and simpler problem environment by ignoring certain aspects of the original problem, (*b*) forms a corresponding problem in the abstract task environment and solves it, (*c*) uses this solution to provide a plan for solving the original problem, and (*d*) translates this plan back into the original task environment and executes it (Newell et al., 1959; Newell & Simon, 1972).

As this description of the planning method indicates, Newell and his colleagues viewed planning as a problem-solving technique that is used to guide action when the original problem is too difficult. In more recent research, planning and problem solving are often used interchangeably or planning is used as a part of the problem-solving process in a manner similar to what Newell et al. intended (see, for example, Dreher & Oerter, 1987; Glass & Holyoak, 1986; Oppenheimer, 1987). Several authors have, however, explicitly distinguished planning from problem solving and consider the former to be a much broader concept than the latter. The relationship between planning and problem solving will be discussed in more detail later but now we will examine more closely Miller et al.'s ideas, which are frequently referred to as having initiated the psychology of planning.

PLANS AND THE STRUCTURE OF BEHAVIOR

The book *Plans and the Structure of Behavior* had a pervasive influence on the investigation of cognitive processes since its appearance in 1960. This was due mainly to the fact that, as Hebb (1960, p. 206) stated, Miller, Galanter, and Pribram had presented "something worth knowing about human beings". Miller et al. proposed the concept of "plan", which is analogous to the program for a computer, to fill the theoretical vacuum between cognition and action. Although they regarded computer simulations of human thought processes to be very promising, they acknowledged that "the reduction of Plans to nothing but programs is still a scientific hypothesis and is still in need of further validation" (p. 16). This brain-computer analogy has since been one of the central problems in artificial intelligence and we will discuss it later in this chapter.

Miller et al. emphasized the description of the structural features of behavior as exemplified by ethologists (Thorpe, 1956; Tinbergen, 1951) and linguists (Carroll, 1953; Chomsky, 1957), and asserted that behavior is organized simultaneously at several levels of complexity. With the hierarchical nature of behavior as axiomatic, they defined a plan as "any hierarchical process in the organism that can control the order in which a sequence of operations is to be performed" (p. 16). A plan could involve anything from a rough sketch of a course of action to a detailed specification of each operation. *It is the plan that controls human information processing and supplies patterns for essential connections between knowledge, evaluation, and action.*

Miller et al. assumed that all behavior is guided by hierarchically organized plans that may include several subplans and further subplans up to the level of motor action. Thus, they suggested that the Plan is the appropriate unit of analysis for behavior at both the molar and the molecular level. They also offered several examples of such analyses by discussing the crucial role of plans in memorizing, problem solving, and language production, as well as in the formation of automatic skills and habits. Furthermore, they suggested that higher-level planning ability (that is, the ability to use plans to construct plans) may be the evolutionary breakthrough separating human beings from other animals.

But how do we construct new plans? Miller et al. proposed that most plans are learned, either through imitation or through verbal instructions from another person. New plans that are not learned are based either on old plans (i.e., we change old plans to fit new contexts) or "metaplans" and "heuristic plans". Metaplans are plans for plan formation that are abstracted from inherited and learned plans in order to lessen the memory requirements for the planner. That is, instead of storing all of the plans that we learn and may need later, we store higher order plans for generating the lower level plans when necessary. Heuristic plans, in turn, are needed when metaplans are unable to produce a solution. Following this line of logic, we would need further plans to form heuristic plans and metaplans, a problem noted by Miller et al. Their solution to this problem involved the idea that heuristic plans are used to produce new heuristic plans and that to construct a general outline of problem solving, a plausible description of the heuristic process is required. This description, the authors anticipated, would be provided by a growing number of artificial intelligence researchers who were interested in developing heuristic methods for computers. A generally accepted account of human heuristic processes, however, is still lacking; Miller et al.'s description of the planning process may have convinced many researchers to focus their attention on plans and their behavioral results instead of planning activity and its motivational and cognitive determinants.

The second central concept in Miller et al.'s description of cognitive processes is "image". They defined images as "all the accumulated knowledge the organism has about itself and its world" (1960, p. 17) and maintained that it "includes everything the organism has learned—his values as well as his facts—organised by whatever concepts, images, or relations he has been able to master" (1960, pp. 17-18). Images and plans are, of course, reciprocally related in several ways. A plan can be learned and stored as an image or as a part of it. The accumulated knowledge stored in images is incorporated into plans to provide a basis for guiding behavior; images can therefore form a part of a plan. Changes in an image can be brought about only by executing plans for gathering, storing, or transforming information. Alternatively, changes in plans can be brought about only by information drawn from images. An image, as Miller et al. use it, consists of much more than just imagery. Images are individuals' private representations of the world and of themselves, and they comprise the knowledge base for all cognitive processing.

Miller et al. suggested that *search* is an adequate representation of most of the information processing that takes place during thinking and problem solving. The search that they conceived of was, naturally, planful. They also suggested that we should distinguish between *problems to prove* and *problems to find*.

A problem to find is what we normally have in mind when we refer to searching: How does one find the topic for a term paper? How does one find a friend in a crowded marketplace? We can solve problems to find by forming and implementing a plan that involves searching for different alternative solutions and selecting between them. As Miller et al. note, this type of plan is more often heuristic and based on cues derived from our knowledge base than it is exhaustive or even strictly systematic; implementing an exhaustive and strictly systematic plan would simply be too laborious for most problems encountered in everyday life. Consider the process of buying a house, for example. How many variables affecting the decision about the type of house to buy and its location can one identify in, say, three minutes? How many different possible combinations can one form from these variables? Clearly, the number of possible combinations is too large for any human being to search through categorically and the ultimate decision made will be based on a limited search or perhaps even on intuition. (Intuition, according to Simon [1992], may be nothing more than the recognition of information already stored in one's knowledge base.) Perhaps the good planners in real-life tasks are those who limit their searches in the most effective way.

A problem to prove is concerned with evaluating the veracity of a statement that could be either true or false. Examples of such problems can be found, for example, in logic, arithmetics, or in games involving strategies. The problem to prove includes a statement of what is given (A) and a statement of what is to be proven (C), and we need to discover the missing step or sequence of steps (B) that leads from (A) to (C). Normally we have to search through a large set of possible Bs to find the correct one. If we want this search to be effective, we need a plan to guide it. This plan is often heuristic at the beginning of the task but becomes more systematic toward the end of the task, when the number of viable alternatives has been limited to a more manageable number. Thus, problems to prove are not necessarily different from problems to find: Both involve a search that is more effective if it is guided by a functional plan.

Miller et al. proposed *prediction* as an alternative paradigm to explain thinking and problem solving. For example, we can predict where to find a lost item and then test the prediction by checking if the item is really there. Or we can predict that a certain sequence of steps constitutes B in a problem to prove and then execute them in order to test that prediction. Miller et al. suggest that a prediction paradigm directs our attention more to the image than to the process of planning, mainly because the prediction is based on a hypothetical image. The test, accordingly, either confirms or refutes that image. They make the additional point that evaluations and judgements often involve the construction of a better image, which is not necessarily based on the execution of a plan. But it can be and we should note that when the construction of a better image is planful, this approach is just another way of explaining the process of searching the path from A to C.

Thus, it seems to us that search and planning are largely interrelated, although distinct, concepts. The use of plans and strategies is often a prerequisite for effective search in many experimental (and real-life) tasks. Accordingly, success in these tasks indicates good planning skills as well as good search skills. In Chapter 5 we will introduce a series of studies that have utilized the search paradigm in exploring components of planning.

Linking evaluations and judgements to images (i.e., to a knowledge base) is also an important point. It implies that the basis for good evaluations and judgements depends on enlarging and perhaps even more importantly, organizing our knowledge base so that it provides the most appropriate images. Older people often make better judgements based on their extensive life experiences. Nevertheless, we all know of at least one person who continuously makes poor judgements and appears unable to learn from negative experiences. Can this be based on poor organization of one's knowledge base? Or is there also, at least in some cases, a significant planning component involved in making evaluations and judgements, one that deals mainly with the search for, and the selection of, the most important features of the situation? We believe that these questions may be of significant relevance to career or marriage counseling, or for understanding prevalent adolescent problems such as rising high school drop-out rates. Perhaps providing information about different approaches and alternatives (or the lack of them) is insufficient for individuals who lack the essential planning skills to make use of such information. An important implication here is that such individuals may be classified as lacking motivation when, in fact, the problem involves a lack of cognitive skills.

Ideas expressed in *Plans and the Structure of Behavior*, though speculative, have proven to be of much heuristic significance for the study of cognitive functions. The book has provided cognitive psychologists with a general frame of reference for investigating strategic behavior and cognitive controls in the deployment of higher mental processes. By introducing the concept of plan, it has revitalized interest in legitimate and significant questions relating to purpose, consciousness, intention, and goal-directed behavior, and has therefore been instrumental in the final split from neobehaviorism. Also, some of the ideas that Miller et al. put forth tentatively later became central issues in planning research. Two of these, the use of search as a paradigm for planning and the emphasis on the importance of understanding the physiological basis of cognitive processes, are discussed in more detail later in this book.

Although Miller et al.'s book was a compelling attempt to conceptualize planning as a cognitive process, their approach was not free of problems. Their definition of a plan lists "hierarchy" and "sequence" as criteria for plans and thus excludes plans that are not hierarchically structured or that do not include a sequence of operations. Do we have such plans? The answer is: yes. Sometimes the entire plan consists of one condition that is not necessarily controlled to any extent by the planner and one action to be taken when that condition is satisfied. Also, as Hayes-Roth and Hayes-Roth (1979) have shown, planning is not necessarily hierarchical in nature. Miller et al.'s definition can also be problematic for developmental psychologists: If hierarchization and sequencing are used as criteria for establishing the existence of planning, developmentally early planful behavior displayed by infants and toddlers has to be excluded or discussed under some other label (as suggested in Chapter 4).

Miller et al. also suggest that all behavior is based on plans. At the same time, they emphasize the role of language in planning. This leads to a disturbing question: Is there, then, no plan (or plans) and accordingly, no behavior, when language is not available (as, for example, in the case of infants)? One can argue, as we do in Chapter 4, that infants do not plan but one cannot similarly argue that they do not behave. Miller et al. did not discuss the role of language in planning from a developmental perspective and consequently, they were unaware of the problematic nature of their definition. Moreover, they provided no discussion of the development of planning that could have addressed these questions.

RECENT IDEAS ON PLANNING

THE OPPORTUNISTIC MODEL OF PLANNING

Hayes-Roth and Hayes-Roth (1979) proposed an "Opportunistic Model of Planning" in their influential paper that discussed the structure of planning as a cognitive process. They defined planning as "the predetermination of a course of action aimed at achieving some goal" (pp. 275-276) and like Newell et al. before them, viewed planning as part of the problem-solving process. For Hayes-Roth and Hayes-Roth, planning represented the first stage of a two-stage problem-solving process. *Control*, the second stage, consisted of "monitoring and guiding the execution of the plan to a successful conclusion" (p. 276).

Based on their analysis of the thinking aloud protocols of college students who performed a hypothetical errand planning task and on a computer simulation of the model, Hayes-Roth and Hayes-Roth concluded that the planning process is largely opportunistic and multidirectional in nature. They argued that new decisions and observations made during the planning process suggest different possibilities for plan development and, as a result of the new information, the planner will revise or even abandon the original plan. This is possible because planning comprises the activities of several cognitive "specialists" which operate in a two-dimensional planning space (time and abstraction level defining the dimensions) on the basis of set condition–action rules. Cognitive specialists operate on a "blackboard" that is divided into five conceptual planes, or levels of abstraction, representing different components of the planning process: *plan, plan abstraction, knowledge base, executive,* and *metaplan.* Each planning process proceeds through a series of "cycles" during which different cognitive specialists suggest actions on the blackboard. At the beginning of each cycle, some (or all) specialists have their conditions satisfied and the executive

> selects one of the invoked specialists to execute its action— that is, to generate a new decision and record it on the blackboard. The new decision invokes additional specialists and the next cycle begins. This process ordinarily continues until: (a) the planner has integrated mutually consistent decisions into a complete plan; and (b) the planner has decided that the existing plan satisfies important evaluation criteria (Hayes-Roth & Hayes-Roth, 1979, p. 291).

In the Opportunistic Model of Planning, a decision made at any level of abstraction can affect subsequent decisions both at higher and lower levels of abstraction. According to Hayes-Roth and Hayes-Roth, this multidirectionality distinguishes the Opportunistic Model from successive refinement models (see, for example, Sacerdoti, 1977) of planning, which emphasize the hierarchical and sequential (i.e., "top-down") nature of planning. The latter is viewed as a special case of opportunistic planning that can manifest under one of the following conditions: (*a*) the problem exhibits an inherent hierarchical structure; (*b*) the problem is well-defined and familiar to the planner; or (*c*) the problem can be solved by the planner's habitual method of problem solving.

Although Hayes-Roth and Hayes-Roth (1979) clearly distinguish between plan formation (that is, planning) and plan execution (i.e., control) at the beginning of their article, their model does not. The task that they used was completely hypothetical and contained no separate execution phase. Thus, for the subjects, the entire problem-solving act consisted of constructing the plan required by the experimenter. From the subjects' perspective, they were engaged in planning-in-action and the task contained no distinction between the plan formation and the plan execution phases. In real-life planning tasks, plan formation and plan execution often occur simultaneously— perhaps in a manner that Hayes-Roth and Hayes-Roth suggested—and any definition of planning that claims to be ecologically valid will need to acknowledge this. Our original plans of action are often sketchy at best and are revised and supplemented several times during execution if this process does not proceed as anticipated or if new information suggests better ways of reaching the same goal (or sometimes, better goals).

A further limitation of the model is that Hayes-Roth and Hayes-Roth, like Newell et al., treat planning as a component of problem solving. As we shall see below, this is too narrow a conceptualization of the planning process.

BLUEPRINTS FOR THINKING

Other new ideas and research on planning have been presented recently in a timely and interesting book, *Blueprints for Thinking*. Friedman, Scholnick and Cocking (1987), the editors of the book, present in one volume a number of articles (many of which will be referred to later in this book) from researchers representing a variety of theoretical and practical approaches to the study of planning. In the introductory chapter, Scholnick and Friedman (1987) suggest that the planning process includes at least the following six functions: forming a representation of the problem, choosing a goal, deciding to plan, formulating a plan, executing and monitoring the plan, and learning from the plan. Scholnick and Cocking also suggest that "[t]o plan is to act simultaneously on three levels: in the reality of a problem, in accordance with an imagined scheme, and in the role of mediator between the scheme and the behavior" (p. 3). Relying on these definitions, they offer an integrative review of the current state of planning research. Drawing from a wide range of sources, they identify the following main concerns and sources of confusion in the existing literature on planning:

1. The concepts of plan and planning have been used to explain many different facets of human functioning, with the result that their definitions have become vague. Specifically, two theorists who use the same terms seldom have the same focus. The vagueness of existing definitions may reflect researchers' failure to specify which of the three levels is being referred to and how these levels are integrated. Scholnick and Cocking (1987)

further suggest that a theory of planning should be comprehensive enough to encompass every level of cognition.

Aside from failing to specify the level being referred to, different analyses of planning tend to emphasize different planning functions and usually only address one or two at a time. Theories that would adequately describe several such functions do not yet exist.

2. Most researchers have treated planning as either a general cognitive skill or as a context-specific activity. Very few have attempted to explain how these different frameworks might be subsumed within one definition. Furthermore, some theorists have regarded planning as a mandatory cognitive activity that we all engage in all of the time and they have, therefore, concentrated on the mechanisms involved in planning. Others, however, have emphasized the voluntary nature of planning and have, accordingly, concentrated on individual differences in whether one decides to plan in the first place. Unfortunately, these two approaches have not yet been merged.

3. Individual differences in planning efficiency have been accounted for either through the number of planning components present and the speed of their execution (that is, by quantitative differences), or through "stylistic variations" that reflect qualitative differences in the ways that individuals plan.

The above observations by Scholnick and Friedman (1987) summarize several of the central problems that one encounters in the planning literature. Planning is an activity that synthesizes several different components and levels of functioning into one scheme. Researchers have seldom agreed about which levels or components should be singled out for discussion. We believe that this state of affairs is a consequence of (a) the lack of a comprehensive theory of planning that would integrate available knowledge from experimental cognitive psychology and allied fields, (b) the prevalent view of planning as equivalent to (or a component of) a problem-solving process, (c) extensive and uncritical reliance on models of computer simulation and artificial intelligence, and (d) the almost total disregard for a neuropsychological basis for planning as a cognitive process. We hope that the remaining chapters in this book will help the vigilant reader to find at least some tentative solutions to the problems identified by Scholnick and Friedman, as well as to detect possible new problems. But before we define planning as a cognitive process in more detail, it is necessary to review briefly some of the central themes and assumptions in current planning research. These include the use of artificial intelligence models, equating planning with problem solving or with the use of a strategy, and the role of metacognition.

RECURRENT THEMES

PLANNING AND ARTIFICIAL INTELLIGENCE MODELS

Since planning research has proliferated with an impetus from artificial intelligence (AI) models of problem solving, at this point it seems appropriate to discuss the adequacy of such models in explaining human cognition. The concept of the computer has certainly advanced our knowledge of human information processing. To equate plans and programs conceptually, however, may be too simplistic. The complexity of the human information-processing system far exceeds that of existing computer programs. Humans can substantially increase their rate of information transmission by altering and reorganizing given information. We can take in information, recode it, store it, and transform it (sometimes even unconsciously). We can also reorganize our knowledge according to changing contextual demands, make decisions, change them, and translate them into action. More importantly, however, we can reflect on this entire process while it is occurring *and* after the fact. Although computer programs have been able to simulate many facets of human information processing, the self-organizing and reflective nature of this processing has proven extremely difficult to reproduce mechanically.

Planning is a self-organizing, reflective process. According to Clancey (1991) AI models have essentially ignored "natural examples of self-organising processes and what kind of complex behaviors they can produce" (p. 258). He continues:

Indeed, we must stop and rethink the rubric of "information processing" that still unites most parts of AI and cognitive science. Perhaps our field betrays too much its origins in the computer industry, with data supplied on cards and each job completed as a neat processing from input to output piles. More generally, what is at stake is our ideas about how models relate to mechanisms and what mechanisms can be built (p. 282).

Reflecting the same sentiments, Black (1991) argues that the computer analogy of the brain is entirely misleading and fails to capture the nature of the neurological activities taking place in the brain. He assures us that the main feature of life systems is not represented by computer models: consider the fact that in life systems, higher levels continually transform the lower, more elementary levels upon which they are based. This is especially true with such higher cognitive functions as complex real-life planning tasks; while planning we are constantly redefining and transforming stimuli, our knowledge base, and the goals of our activity. This bidirectional, and sometimes nonlinear, relationship does not characterize existing computer models of planning, although some of them (for example, the Opportunistic Model of Planning) do capture aspects of it.

Advocating a Neuropsychological Connection

Over 20 years ago Luria (1973a) warned that psychological principles cannot be represented by mechanical models and that when used, such models "do not help, but rather hinder, the advancement of [a] truly scientific knowledge of the brain as the organ of the mind" (p. 15). The present authors' view is that the study of human cognitive functions must involve the discovery of neuropsychological and neurophysiological models of higher mental processes, and planning is, preeminently, one such process. Information processing is a function of the brain. Hence, if we desire to understand it, we must attempt to comprehend how it occurs in the brain. However, "[p]sychological problems may not be solved by making measurements in the brain, but some more modest aim may be accomplished; a psychological analysis that can stand up to the neurological evidence is certainly better than one that cannot" (Miller et al., 1960, p. 196).

Thus, we can conclude with some certainty that computer metaphors have as yet failed to account for human information processing at both cognitive and neurophysiological levels of analysis.

Even the most ardent proponents of computer simulations of human cognition (see, for example, Simon, 1990, 1992) have acknowledged that computer models and neurophysiology are "miles apart". This does not, however, mean that computer models have no value in explaining, or could not become better approximators of, human cognitive processes. What we must keep in mind is that "reductive microdeterminism" (Sperry, 1993), be it in neurocellular–physiochemical terms or in a programming language, cannot provide a full account of human activity without considering the higher order forces that affect it. In other words, we have to consider downward determinism as well as upward determinism in any discussion of causality (Sperry, 1993). This downward determinism, which includes environmental and cultural variables, is still largely absent from artificial intelligence models of planning.

Artificial Intelligence and Learning

The preceding treatment of artificial intelligence (AI) may have been somewhat harsh and perhaps not entirely fair, since there is much similarity between artificial intelligence and classical learning theory approaches to planning. Anderson (1993) made a bold attempt to combine the central concepts of the AI approach with animal and human learning. Following his initiative, the relationship between artificial intelligence and learning will be examined in some detail.

The major difficulty in accepting AI is perhaps that its new jargon or terminology appears to be independent of the language of psychology developed since Wilhelm Wundt and William James. We believe that AI concepts could become much more acceptable if they were understood within the context of the history of psychology. For example, when we describe planning a course of action, whether it involves a rat in a typical maze or a human being solving a puzzle such as the Tower of Hanoi or Crack-the-Code (see Chapter 7), three concepts at the core of AI are used.

The first concept is that of *problem state*, which can refer to some external state of affairs and/or to the internal coding of that state of affairs (Anderson, 1993). Thus, problem state is really a substitute concept for the stimulus and how it is conceptualized by the learner. Both the physical arrangement of the learning situation (i.e., stimuli) and the way in which the subject conceives of these arrangements (i.e., interpretation) can define the AI concept of a problem state. Although the learning situation, as physically arranged, does not change as the individual acquires knowledge about it, the knowledge itself undergoes changes. In other words, the individual's interpretation of the stimulus and its context changes. Such changes are visible in the organism's behavior as traditionally shown in the experiments by Hull, Tolman, and Guthrie, and in the earlier work of Thorndike (see, for example, Hilgard & Bower, 1966). In sum, the problem state seems to refer to the individual's representations of the learning task and these are changing continuously as a result of learning.

The second key concept in AI problem solving is *operator*. Operators are actions that can transform one problem state into another (Anderson, 1993). In more familiar psychological language, operator refers to the activities that are necessary for learning. For human beings, much of these activities are internal, involving reflection and hypothesis testing that proceed covertly and change the conceptualization of the problem at hand. In fact, planning is the chief covert mental activity involved in solving many intellectual problems.

The final central AI concept is *problem space*. Problem space is defined by possible states and operators that the individual can use to move toward the goal state. The concept refers to the entire arrangement of the learning problem: the blind alleys in a maze that have to be traversed and eliminated, or the moves in a puzzle that reduce the distance between the starting point and the goal. The classical learning theories of Tolman and Hull, for example, discuss goals, drives, vicarious trial-and-error behavior, and fractional anticipatory goal responses, all of which concern the reduction of the distance between the starting point and the goal. According to Anderson (1993), the most important method that humans possess for reducing this distance is means-ends analysis. This is another AI term that has also been expressed in traditional learning theories, especially in the concept of successive approximations whereby an animal is taught to reach a goal.

Anderson (1993) advocates the point of view that most intellectual and motor tasks may be conceptualized as problem solving (i.e., finding a solution to a given problem). We may be capable of teaching an animal how to reach a goal but a rational program, such as a means-ends analysis, does not always reflect how either an animal or a human problem solver actually plans and solves a problem. The reason for this is that not all of our plans are rational. Instead, there is a significant amount of unpredictability in how an animal or a human being will undertake to solve a problem. This is particularly true with human problem solving and planning: A significant amount of unpredictability and uncertainty is often present. This is popularly referred to as free will.

Is Planning Nothing More Than Problem Solving?

As mentioned earlier, several authors have considered planning to be a part of the problem-solving process or one method of solving problems when the context requires it. Our own belief about the relationship between problem solving and planning, however, is almost opposite to this position: Planning is a more pervasive, general regulating process than problem solving, with problem solving being a part of a planning process.

Moreover, planning includes components that are not necessarily present in problem solving. One of these components is anticipation. Greeno, Riley, and Gelman (1984) have explicitly emphasized anticipation of action programs as the core component in planning. According to these authors, planning entails "the procedures that recognise goals of different types during planning, that search for action schemata with consequences that match goals that have been recognised, and that determine when planning is successfully completed" (p. 99). Thus, planning involves the generation of anticipatory strategies. This view was also shared by Anderson (1993, p. 167): "If it can be shown that a system reorders a preferred sequence of actions in anticipation of a goal conflict, then that system is engaged in planning". Anticipation inherent in the initial representation of a goal and procedural knowledge of action components also characterize planning in the description of plans provided by Schank and Abelson (1977).

Anticipatory models are highly similar to Miller et al.'s (1960) description of planning discussed earlier. Planning can, however, also include the anticipation or creation of problems *themselves*, as well as the sequence of actions or goals. In other words, planning is oriented toward the future, whereas problem solving is oriented toward solving existing problems (i.e., it is oriented toward the present). A good planner selects and manipulates her or his environment in order to create the most appropriate problems.

The future orientation of planning is also present in Kreitler and Kreitler's (1987) distinction between planning and problem solving. They suggest that planning differs from problem solving in three ways. First, planning refers to the cognitive construction of a behavior program that involves one or more steps, whereas problem solving refers to the execution of these programs (i.e., plans), the evaluation of their adequacy, or sometimes only to the motor manipulation required to solve a task. Second, planning always refers to a future action, whereas problem solving may deal with issues that have nothing to do with action or the future. Last, when we plan, we are specifically trying to discover a way of doing something (i.e., the question is *how* to do or attain something). Problem solving, in turn, may also deal with other questions such as, *why* something is the way that it is, *what* the possible *outcomes* of some event are, or *what* the *purpose* of a particular occasion is.

Kreitler and Kreitler (1987) add that these different features of planning and problem solving make for differences in at least some of the cognitive processes involved in each (see also Ashman & Conway, 1989).

Kreitler and Kreitler's (1987) description, however, includes certain confusions that need to be clarified. One of these concerns the motor aspect of planning. The authors seem to suggest that planning occurs entirely "in the head", whereas problem solving can also involve motor manipulation. The question, then, is: Does planning involve procedural knowledge and problem solving involve declarative knowledge (i.e., the usual distinction between how, on the one hand, and what and why, on the other)? We do not believe that it is useful to separate the two concepts solely on the basis of purely mental or motor actions. As will become clear from the model of planning proposed in Chapter 2, motor functions can constitute part of the output or response system of the individual and may require complex planning and programming. For example, when an individual is reading single words, planning is particularly important after phonological coding of the word, when s/he is assembling pronunciation and is preparing to articulate the word. Thus, the reader may know how to decode a printed word phonologically but s/he may not be able to pronounce it without a certain amount of planning to produce the sequence of sounds. Similarly, in the problem solving that occurs while doing arithmetic the organization of procedures for solving the problem certainly requires planning. In fact, individual differences in planning tests correlate significantly with efficiency in carrying out arithmetic operations (Das, Naglieri, & Kirby, 1994).

Despite the conceptual differences discussed above, planning and problem solving are similar enough in actual experimental studies that we can, with some qualifications, draw from the problem solving literature in order to understand planning. What must be kept in mind, however, is that planning may include components that are not necessarily present in problem solving and that some forms of problem solving may not demand planning. In the next chapter, a model of planning is presented that includes problem solving as a component and that clarifies the relationship between both concepts.

PLANNING AND STRATEGIES

The concepts of plan and strategy are often used interchangeably. When they introduced the term *strategy* into cognitive psychology, Bruner et al. (1956) defined it as "a pattern of decision in the acquisition and utilisation of information that serves to meet certain objectives" (p. 54). They also noted that strategies are not fixed and that they are presumably learned. In addition, they emphasized that a strategy may not be conscious and that whether it is conscious or not is largely irrelevant.

Miller et al. (1960) considered strategies to be molar units of behavior and viewed tactics as molecular units. In their hierarchical description of human functioning, a properly executed strategy guides the construction of an effective sequence of tactics and the search for and selection of strategies is, in turn, guided by plans. Kirby (1984) maintained essentially the same distinctions in his analysis of planning. He argued that plans are undoubtedly hierarchical in that one plan may call for the execution of a subplan which can, in turn, be part of another plan (and so forth). According to this view, strategies are equivalent to subplans but because of the hierarchical nature of the entire process, they can also be viewed as plans at some level of analysis.

Strategic variables have received the most scrutiny in memory research (see, for example, Atkinson & Shiffrin, 1967). Some of the memory strategies that have been shown to affect performance include verbal coding of nonverbal stimuli, rehearsal to maintain information for short time intervals, organizing and categorizing items to be remembered, and elaborating the relations among items either verbally or with the use of imagery. These strategies play an important role in enhancing the memory system's limited capacity, especially in terms of the acquisition and retention of new information. They are also important because their use requires planning, which involves the individual's control of their selection, regulation, and monitoring (Spitz & Borys, 1984).

In conclusion, we could say that plans are higher units of analysis than strategies. But strategies can also be conceptualized as plans. For example, different memory strategies can be conceptualized as plans to be implemented, either consciously or unconsciously. If we then expand our focus to include the selection of different strategies for different tasks, strategies can now be conceptualized as subplans. Using the terms strategy and plan interchangeably is thus allowed, as long as the formation of "strategies" is consistent with the definition of planning as a cognitive process. This is an important qualifier because we believe that some strategies can be formed without the individual ever being conscious of them (e.g., the preference for one information coding method over another [see Chapter 2]), whereas the individual is conscious of plans at least at some point in their development.

METACOGNITION

Awareness and knowledge of cognition are relevant to all aspects of the planning process (Das et al., 1994). Conscious planning implies that the individual is aware and capable of regulating his or her cognitive processes. In this sense, metacognition is a prerequisite for planning.

Several authors (see, for example, Brown, Bransford, Ferrara, & Campione, 1983; Jarman, Vavrik, & Walton, 1995; Kitchener, 1983) have noted that there is no generally accepted definition of metacognition, apart from the partially redundant statement that metacognition refers to one's knowledge about cognition. Brown et al. (1983) argue that confusion with the use of the term metacognition stems from two sources: (*a*) it is often difficult to distinguish between what is meta and what is cognitive; and (*b*) metacognition is used to refer to two different areas of research, namely, *knowledge about cognition* and *the regulation of cognition*. These two forms of metacognition are closely related yet distinguishable (see also, Lawson, 1980, 1984). Knowledge about cognition refers to relatively stable, stateable, fallible, and late-developing information that we have about our own cognitive processes and those of others. Regulation of cognition, however, refers to a cluster of activities that we use to control learning and other cognitive activities. These activities include, for example, *planning* (i.e., predicting outcomes, scheduling strategies, etc.), *monitoring* (i.e., testing, revising, etc.), and *checking* outcomes (i.e., evaluating the outcome and the process, etc.). Brown et al. suggest that the term metacognition should be limited to its original usage (i.e., knowledge about cognition), whereas the regulation of cognition should be discussed using only processing terms.

We agree with this distinction between knowledge about and regulation of cognition. When we use the term metacognition in this book, we are referring to the knowledge that an individual has of his or her cognitive states and processes. Our definition of planning, however, is considerably broader than that of Brown et al. Perhaps metacognitive knowledge should be seen as part of the knowledge base from which planning operates, whereas the process of planning includes the regulation of cognitive processes (e.g., the allocation of attention between different components of a task).

The absence of metacognition can frequently explain the failure of instruction. Students are commonly taught content (i.e., knowledge, particularly declarative knowledge) and how to do things (i.e., skills and strategies, or procedural knowledge). What they often fail to acquire is an understanding of why that knowledge is important, as well as how and when it should be employed. In short, they lack metacognitive knowledge about when to use their declarative and procedural knowledge and are therefore unlikely to see the value of that knowledge or be able to retain it. Paris, Newman, and McVey (1982) have provided a good example of this process. They taught seven- and eight-year-old children a strategy (i.e., a plan) for remembering numbers, which improved their immediate performance on the task. After four days, the children were tested again. Those who had been taught only the strategy reverted to their previous approach and exhibited poor performance similar to that of a control group who had not been taught the strategy. A third group of children, who had been taught the strategy and who had been given an explanation of its usefulness, were the only group to use the strategy and maintain a high level of performance. We believe that teaching planning (i.e., the formation and selection of strategies), as opposed to readymade plans, should also lead to positive results because it adds a metacognitive dimension to the task.

Two aspects of metacognition should be mentioned in order to strengthen its links with planning. The first is that metacognition, like planning, requires motivation. An individual does not engage in metacognitive activities without a purpose and a need. The second aspect concerns cognitive development. Metacognition appears to involve two stages of development (Kirby & Moore, 1987). The first stage appears at approximately age 5, when children begin to take conscious control of their strategies or thinking. The second stage emerges at approximately age 12, when children begin to take a more abstract, analytical, and systematic approach to controlling their thinking. These two stages correspond to major transitions in cognitive development: from preoperations to concrete operations, and from concrete to formal operations, respectively. As we shall see later, these stages also correspond to significant changes in the functioning of the frontal lobes, which are often depicted as the "organ" of planning.

2

PLANNING AND THE PASS THEORY

During recent years a comprehensive model of cognitive processing has been advanced with planning as a central concept (Das, 1973, 1980, 1984a, 1984b; Das & Heemsbergen, 1983; Das, Kirby, & Jarman, 1975, 1979; Naglieri & Das, 1990). The Planning, Attention-Arousal, Simultaneous, and Successive (PASS) cognitive processing model is described as a modern theory of ability that is based on A. R. Luria's (1966, 1970, 1973a, 1980) analyses of brain structures and functioning. It also incorporates ideas from more recent cognitive psychological research. Prior to introducing the PASS theory in more detail, however, we need to examine briefly the brain and its structure.

THE BRAIN

The structural foundation of the working mind is the brain. The brain is contained within the skull. When we open the skull we first encounter the hard tissue that shields the brain, which is referred to as the dura mater or hard matter. The next membrane beneath the dura mater is the arachnoid or cobweb, and the final membrane is called the pea mater or tender matter. The cerebrospinal fluid is enclosed between the arachnoid and the pea mater, and fills all of the brain's irregular crevices. The entire volume of cerebrospinal fluid, however, is less than that of a teacup.

We actually possess two brains, referred to as the left and right hemispheres and to the naked eye they appear identical. Along the center of the brain, dividing the brain into two halves, is a deep ditch referred to as the longitudinal sulcus. It travels from the front to the back portion of the brain. A second important sulcus, or ditch, is the Sylvian fissure, which is located on both hemispheres. Next, there is the central fissure, which travels downward from the top of the brain over the outer portion of the hemispheres and joins the Sylvian fissure. The reason that we make note of these fissures is to divide the brain, which is otherwise continuous, into three main regions (displayed in Figure 2.1).

Figure 2.1
The Main Regions of the Brain

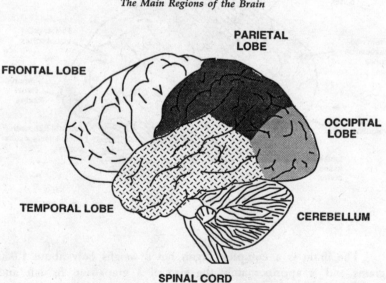

These regions are: (*a*) the frontal lobe, which includes that portion of the brain located in front of the central fissure; (*b*) the parietal and occipital lobes, which are the areas behind the central fissure; and (*c*) the temporal lobe, which is the area below the Sylvian fissure. (The frontal lobe will be an important topic in the remainder of this chapter and in the next chapter.) Anterior to the central sulcus, the frontal lobe contains the precentral gyrus, which includes the motor cortex. Further forward is the premotor cortex and still more anterior are the prefrontal fibers or prefrontal lobes. Figure 2.2 identifies some of the central functional regions within the frontal, temporal, occipital, and parietal lobes.

Figure 2.2
Details of Functional Regions within the Frontal, Temporal, Occipital, and Parietal Lobes

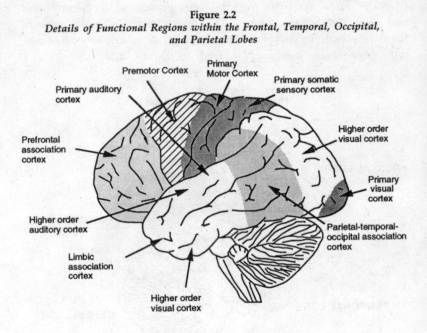

The brain is a complex organ but it weighs only about 1,000 grams and is approximately the size of a grapefruit. Its left and right hemispheres are connected by the corpus callosum, which is a large bundle of fibers. The base of the brain consists of such structures as the medulla oblongata, which regulates autonomic functions such as respiration, blood circulation, and digestion. The cerebellum, which coordinates movement, lies below the brain. Inside the brain is the limbic system, a collection of tissues and fibers that are related to emotional behavior and are even involved in long-term memory.

Communication between various neurons in different areas of the' brain can occur through many types of transmitters. The first neurotransmitter was identified over 70 years ago and at present, 50 different types of neurotransmitters have been identified. An important fact to remember is that the sensory systems are organized in a hierarchical manner, a point that is elaborated below. Another important point is that information does not travel as a complete entity along a single neuronal pathway. Instead, different features of a single percept are processed simultaneously (i.e., in parallel) rather than along single pathways.

THE PASS THEORY OF
INFORMATION PROCESSING

Luria (1966, 1970, 1973a, 1980) described human cognitive processes within a framework of three functional units. The function of the first unit is the regulation of cortical arousal and attention; the second unit codes information using simultaneous and successive processes; and the third unit provides for planning, self-monitoring, and structuring of cognitive activities. Luria's work on the functional aspects of brain structures formed the basis of the PASS model and was used as a blueprint for defining the important components of human intellectual competence.

The first functional unit of the brain, the attention-arousal system, is located mainly in the brain stem, the diencephalon, and the medial regions of the cortex (Luria, 1973a). This unit provides the brain with the appropriate level of arousal or cortical tone, and "directive and selective attention" (Luria, 1973a, p. 273). That is, when a multidimensional stimulus array is presented to a subject and s/he is required to pay attention to only one dimension, the inhibition of responding to other (often more salient) stimuli and the allocation of attention to the central dimension depends on the resources of the first functional unit. Luria stated that optimal conditions of arousal are needed before the more complex forms of attention involving "selective recognition of a particular stimulus and inhibition of responses to irrelevant stimuli" occur (Luria, 1973a, p. 271). Moreover, only when an individual is sufficiently aroused and when attention is adequately focused can s/he utilize processes in the second and third functional units.

The first functional unit is not an autonomous system but works in cooperation with, and is regulated by, higher systems of the cerebral cortex, which receive and process information from the external world and determine an individual's dynamic activity (Luria, 1973a). In other words, this unit has a reciprocal relationship with the cortex: it influences the tone of the cortex and is itself being influenced by the regulatory effects of the cortex. This is possible through the ascending and descending systems of the reticular formation, which transmit impulses from lower parts of the brain to the cortex and vice versa (Luria, 1973a). For the PASS theory this means that attention-arousal and planning are necessarily correlated since the former is often under the conscious control of Planning. In sum, our plan of behavior dictates the allocation of our limited attentional resources.

Luria's description of the second functional unit of the brain follows the work of Sechenov. This unit is responsible for the reception, coding, and storage of information arriving from the external (and partially from the internal) environment through sensory receptors. It is located in the lateral regions of the neocortex, on the convex surface of the hemispheres, of which it occupies the posterior regions, including the visual (occipital), auditory (temporal) and general sensory (parietal) regions (Luria, 1973a). Luria described "two basic forms of integrative activity of the cerebral cortex" (Luria, 1966, p. 74) that take place in this unit: simultaneous and successive processing. Simultaneous processing is associated with the occipital—parietal areas of the brain (Luria, 1966) and its essential feature is surveyability, that is, each element is related to every other element at any given time (Naglieri, 1989). For example, in order to produce a diagram correctly when given the instruction, "draw a triangle above a square that is to the left of a circle under a cross", the relationships among the different shapes must be correctly comprehended. Successive processing is associated with the fronto-temporal areas of the brain (Luria, 1973a) and involves the integration of stimuli into a specific serial order (Luria, 1966) where each component is related to the next component. That is, in successive synthesis, "each link integrated into a series can evoke only a particular chain of successive links following each other in serial order" (Luria, 1966, p. 77). For example, successive processes are involved in the decoding and production of syntagmatic aspects of language and speech articulation.

The third functional unit of the brain is located in the prefrontal areas of the frontal lobes of the brain (Luria, 1980). Luria stated that "the frontal lobes synthesize the information about the outside worlds . . . and are the means whereby the behavior of the organism is regulated in conformity with the effect produced by its actions" (p. 263). Planning processes that take place in this unit provide for the programming, regulation, and verification of behavior, and are responsible for behaviors such as asking questions, solving problems, and self-monitoring (Luria, 1973a). Other responsibilities of the third functional unit include the regulation of voluntary activity, conscious impulse control, and various linguistic skills such as spontaneous conversation. The third functional unit provides for the most complex aspects of human behavior, including personality and consciousness (Das, 1980). As Luria (1973b, p. 118) states:

> The frontal lobes of the brain are the last acquisition of the evolutionary process and occupy nearly one-third of the human hemispheres . . . . They are intimately related to the reticular formation of the brain stem, being densely supplied with ascending and descending fibers . . . . They have intimate connections with the motor cortex and with the structures of the second block . . . their structures become mature only during the fourth to fifth year of life, and their development makes a rapid leap during the period which is of decisive significance for the first forms of conscious control of behavior.

The PASS theory provides a model, shown in Figure 2.3, for conceptualizing human intellectual competence and is a blend of neuropsychological, cognitive, and psychometric approaches. The PASS theory has lead to operational definitions of its constructs and an understanding of the structural architecture of processing (Naglieri & Das, 1990) that allows for the identification of good measures of each PASS process. Some of these measures are introduced in detail later in this book.

Figure 2.3
The PASS Model of Cognitive Processes

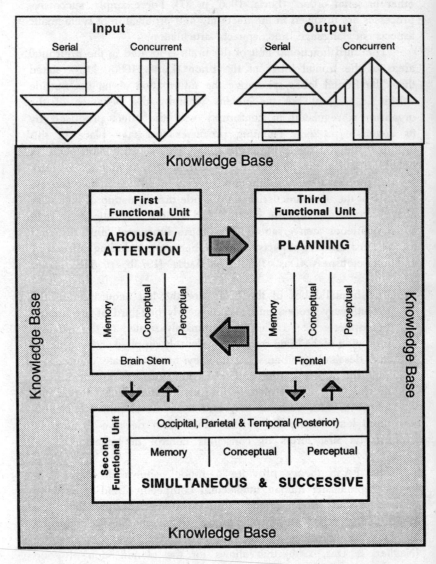

As depicted in Figure 2.3, planning processes are closely connected with attention, on the one hand, and with simultaneous and successive processing, on the other. In assessing an individual's information-processing skills, planning processes are needed when a test requires that the individual make decisions about how to solve a problem; execute an approach; activate attentional, simultaneous, and successive processes; monitor the effectiveness of the approach; and modify the approach as needed. Planning processes are also involved when a person is asked to decide how to perform a test and these processes are inhibited when strict rules about how to perform are imposed. For example, writing a composition involves generation of a plan, organization of ideas, control over what is presented and when it is presented, examination of the preliminary product, and modification of the plan so that the final result is consistent with the goal. Planning processes allow the person to ,guide the course of activity and to utilize attentional, simultaneous, and successive processes, as well as the base of knowledge, in order to achieve the goal. In this sense, we can say that planning is a superstructure in relation to other components of the PASS theory.

Knowledge base is an integral component of the PASS model and as a result, processes are always embedded within this dimension. The base of knowledge included in Figure 2.3 is intended to represent all information that an individual has obtained from his or her cultural, educational, and social settings. In a sense, the knowledge base determines the form of mental activity undertaken by an individual. Children's use of language to "analyze, generalize, and encode experience" (Luria, 1976, p. 9) is a critical determinant of the knowledge base because mental processes cannot develop apart from appropriate forms of social life. The importance of social interactions is perhaps most clearly presented by Luria (1976, p. 133) when he states that "the significance of schooling lies not just in the acquisition of new knowledge, but in the creation of new motives and formal modes of discursive verbal and logical thinking divorced from immediate practical experience". This statement emphasizes the role of knowledge, as well as planning processes (for example, in the creation of motives), in human functioning. Recognizing the importance of the base of knowledge obtained from all sources (formal as well as informal, practical as well as theoretical, etc.), we have incorporated this component into the PASS model.

The PASS model views planning as a functional system that is very similar to the concept of activity discussed by Leontjev (1978, 1979). In the following section we will define planning within this framework and try to provide an integrated picture of the nature of planning as a cognitive activity.

A DEFINITION OF PLANNING

Thus far we have already discussed several definitions of planning. Newell et al. (1959) saw planning as problem solving in a simplified, abstracted problem space. Miller et al. (1960) defined plans as hierarchical control processes. For Hayes-Roth and Hayes-Roth (1979), planning consisted of anticipating a goal-directed course of action. Scholnick and Friedman (1987) included six components (i.e., forming a representation of the problem, choosing a goal, deciding to plan, formulating a plan, executing and monitoring the plan, and learning from the plan) and three levels of functioning (i.e., in the reality of a problem, in accordance with an imagined scheme, and in the role of mediator between the scheme and behavior) in their definition of the planning process.

We have also argued that planning can be a more pervasive regulatory process than problem solving. It is oriented toward the future and may include the creation and selection of problems, as well as the anticipation of a sequence of actions to solve them. Instead of being a hierarchical and linear process, planning is often nonlinear and revisionary in nature, and the formation and execution of a plan can occur simultaneously. Planning is a self-organizing, reflective process that the individual is conscious of at least at some point in its development and it requires motivation and metacognitive skills. It is an activity that integrates several different components and levels of functioning into one schema and is a uniquely human function with close connections to speech and language. But the question emerges: How can we integrate all of this information into one definition of planning as a cognitive process?

We should begin by stating that planning is an intrapsychological process that is mediated by some symbolic, or sign, system. We believe that the most powerful symbolic system is language and therefore, human planning is, more often than not, verbally mediated. The mediated structure of planning means that an auxiliary stimulus, such as a word (Luria, 1982), always acts as a mediating factor between environmental stimuli and an individual's response. In other words, when we are engaged in planning, we will form a mental representation of the situation and our actions with the help of words (or other symbols) prior to actually doing something.

As a mediational process, planning is uniquely human and falls within the category of "higher cognitive functions" (Vygotsky, 1986). Higher cognitive functions are, at least to some degree, derivatives of the interpsychological processes that a child participates in during his or her development. Planning therefore has social origins, that is, we learn most of our plans from other, more capable, planners. Moreover, the decision to plan in certain situations and not in others may already be socially determined and individual differences in engaging in planning may reflect social norms and accumulated knowledge about the appropriateness of planning within that context (Goodnow, 1987). Furthermore, planning is influenced by its location in the frontal lobes of the brain and it therefore also has psychophysiological origins. Both the mediational structure of planning and its dependence on the functioning of the frontal lobes of the brain imply that planning cannot occur in very young children (i.e., not before the regulative function of language has developed and the frontal lobes have matured). Luria (1959, 1973a) indicates that both changes occur at approximately the same time, at ages 4 or 5.

THREE LEVELS OF PLANNING

We suggest that a fertile way of conceptualizing planning and its relationship to such closely related concepts as problem solving and strategies is to consider how planning relates to the three levels of analysis—activity, action, and operation—as introduced by Leontjev (1978, 1979).

At the level of *activity*, planning can be conceptualized as a method of realizing or aiming toward one's general life goals and motives, such as self-fulfilment, self-improvement, education, career development, or planning for a retired life. This means that "activity-planning" is future oriented. As an activity, planning is a molar unit of analysis that can be used to explain an individual's behavior in general. For example, plans for a life after retirement will provide a framework within which a person's behavior can be explained and understood. At this end of the continuum, when our mental activity has an objective or goal, planning appears as a separate activity distinct from imagery. The function of activity-planning is to mediate between an individual's life goals and the external, objective world. In order to do this, activity-planning entails components that are not necessarily present in other forms of planning. The components unique to activity-planning include selection and shaping of one's environments so that they maximally support, or minimally impede, the fulfilment of one's life goals. Problem finding, or the creation and definition of relevant problems that need solution, is also unique to activity-planning. Other possible components of activity-planning, such as forming a representation of external and internal variables that may influence goal attainment, choosing subgoals, and anticipating the course of action that is needed to realize the goals and subgoals, can also be present in planning as an action, which is discussed next.

Action-planning is equivalent to problem solving. While activity-planning is best understood as movement toward realizing one's general life goals, action-planning aims at achieving a particular goal or solving a particular problem. Everyday examples of action-planning include scheduling daily meetings, running errands efficiently, or planning a supper for relatives coming over. Problems and goals of action plans can be components of activity-plans as well. For example, if a general life goal is to obtain a secure and well-paying profession, then the activity-plan may involve such components as deciding upon the most suitable educational institution, financing one's studies, and finding the right type of employment. Action-planning can involve forming a mental representation of the problem, the (external and internal) constraints on planning, the goal, and the course of action to be taken (i.e., formulating a plan in advance), as well as executing the resulting plan and monitoring the whole process.

But action-planning can also be an opportunistic process, or "planning-in-action", when task demands or the planner's skills favor this approach (Hayes-Roth & Hayes-Roth, 1979; Rogoff, Gauvain, & Gardner, 1987). When planning-in-action is chosen, the main components of planning involve continuous evaluations and revisions of plans while they are being implemented. The main feature of action-planning is that it emerges as a response to a given situation or stimuli and is therefore oriented toward the present as well as the future.

At the level of *operations*, plans are equivalent to strategies and tactics, and consist of working toward the solution of a problem (or a part of it) in accordance with task-imposed constraints (i.e., meeting environmental conditions). Everyday examples of operation-plans would include locating a book in a library or using household machines and computers. The main feature of an operation-plan is that it needs to satisfy the specific conditions associated with the task; consequently, it is oriented towards the present. Operation-planning involves forming a representation of the task and conditions, choosing the possible operations to be undertaken, and regulating behavior accordingly. Because the goal, or the end-result, is often given, operation-planning involves forming a representation of the task and conditions, choosing the possible operations to be undertaken, and then executing these steps. Thus, operation-planning can include all the components of action-planning identified above. Two differences, however, should be noted: due to increased environmental constraints, operation-planning allows for less revisions, and the process of choosing between possible operations or ways to proceed is not necessarily conscious if we have available "prepackaged information" (Scholnick & Friedman, 1993), that is, automated tactics or strategies that are associated with positive outcomes. For example, the Visual Search task (see Chapter 5 for description) can be solved efficiently by utilizing visual search strategies that are already automated due to practice with real-life visual search tasks such as locating a friend in a crowd or car keys on a front lawn. When a task allows for only one possible method of proceeding, then planning entails finding that method and executing it. At this end of the continuum, planning disappears when the task imposes both the goal and the operations required, and the subject is allowed no degrees of freedom.

According to the definition that we have outlined, planning and plan are generic terms that refer to any of the three levels of analysis, whereas problem solving refers mainly to the action or operation levels of analysis. Strategies and tactics are only involved at the operation level of analysis. It should also be noted that our conceptualization of *activity* is more in line with that of Vygotsky (see, for example, Kozulin, 1986a) and emphasizes the role of symbolic cognitive activity rather than material activity which was stressed by Leontjev.

GOALS AND PLANS

Our definition of planning also implies that we need to define both the goal state and the problem state during planning. Is it possible for a plan to have a goal state and not a problem state? Or vice versa? The well-structured experimental planning tasks that psychologists like to use (and we are no exception) often have clear goal and problem states, with only a limited number of possible solutions. In contrast, real-life planning tasks can be "ill-structured". They may have a goal state that changes several times during the planning process or the goal may not be conscious or readily apparent to the individual at the beginning of the planning process. Still, there is at least some form of goal or subgoal present if we engage in planning; otherwise, we are not planning but merely reacting or shifting aimlessly from one situation or scheme to another. The subgoal might be as trivial as finding a pen and paper when the still (for the most part) undefined goal is to write fiction. We cannot think of a plan without a goal. But is there always a problem state? A goal without a problem state does not require planning. Therefore, if we have a need to plan in the first place, we need to assume both a goal and a problem state; otherwise, the motivational basis of planning is absent.

The vast majority of the planning literature that will be reviewed in the following chapters will focus on action-planning and operation-planning, and on the formulation of a plan in advance rather than on opportunistic planning. Unfortunately, activity-planning has not received the attention that it deserves despite its relevance for understanding human ,behavior.

3

THE NEUROPSYCHOLOGY OF PLANNING

In order to understand planning as a cognitive process, it is useful to consider in more detail its neurological basis in the brain. Planning is clearly associated with the frontal lobes, especially the prefrontal cortex, as described in the previous chapter. Neuroanatomically, this is a significant finding. The prefrontal area has the largest number of connections with other parts of the brain, including the parietal–temporal and occipital lobes, which are responsible for information coding (simultaneous and successive processing), and subcortical areas, which are responsible for the maintenance of arousal. Given these connections, it is reasonable to assume that at a cognitive level, planning can exert control over other cognitive functions.

Luria suggested that higher mental processes, such as planning, are "organised in systems of concertedly working zones, each of which performs its role in complex functional systems and which may be localised in completely different and often far distant areas of the brain" (Luria, 1973a, p. 31). The three functional units of the brain work in concert to produce mental activity. This cooperation at the cognitive level is depicted by two-way arrows in Figure 2.3. It should be emphasized that although planning is a frontal lobe function, this does not mean that the frontal lobes are capable of independently supporting such complex activity. The following sections will explain how different areas of the brain are interconnected as well as describe in more detail the functions of the frontal lobes.

THE STRUCTURE OF THE FRONTAL LOBES

The frontal lobes have been subdivided in various ways in the neuropsychological literature. Stuss and Benson (1986), for example, divided the frontal lobes into three surface areas: lateral, medial, and inferior (or orbital). On the lateral surface, the frontal lobe is defined as the entire brain area lying in front of the central sulcus and above the lateral fissure. Medially frontal lobes surround the anterior section of the corpus callosum and their posterior region is defined by an imaginary line dropped from the medial portion of the central sulcus to the corpus callosum. From an inferior viewpoint, the temporal lobes form the lateral–posterior borders. In the Broadmann system of segmenting the cortex (Figure 3.1), the areas for the three frontal surfaces are as follows: The lateral surface contains Broadmann areas 4, 6, 8–12, and 43–47; the medial surface consists of areas 6, 8–12, 24, 25, 32, and 33; and the inferior surface includes areas 10–15, 25, and 47 (Stuss & Benson, 1986).

For the purposes of understanding planning, a functional division of the brain is relevant. It relates to Luria's primary, secondary, and tertiary zones, and in this context, Broadmann numbers are useful. For instance, area 4 represents the primary motor area (i.e., the primary zone of the frontal cortex), which is the final cortical motor command area. The premotor area (i.e., the secondary zone of the frontal cortex) is designated by areas 6 and 8. These areas prepare motor programs that will be executed by the primary motor area. One section of area 8, the posterior region of the middle frontal gyrus, contains the motor area for eye movements. Areas 44 (secondary) and 45 (tertiary), which, together, are better known as Broca's area, are considered to represent the motor memories of speech patterns. The prefrontal cortex (i.e., the tertiary zone of the frontal cortex) is represented by areas 9–15, 46, and 47 (Stuss & Benson,

Figure 3.1
Broadmann's Cytoarchitectonic Map of the Brain

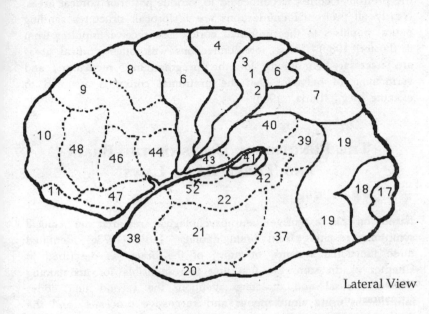

Lateral View

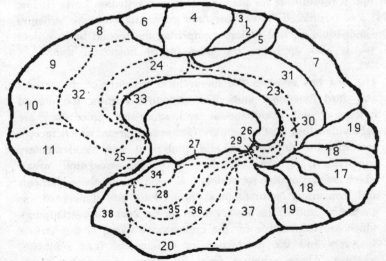

Medial View

1986). Broadly speaking, the functions associated with these areas are the topic of this book.

Aside from the rich thalamic connections mentioned above, the prefrontal cortex is connected to various posterior cortical areas. Nearly all prefrontal connections are reciprocal: structures sending neural impulses to the prefrontal cortex also receive impulses from it (Fuster, 1989). These interconnections with other cortical areas are necessary conditions for the programming, regulation, and verification of behavior that the prefrontal cortex is assumed to execute (e.g., Luria, 1966).

THE FUNCTIONAL UNITS OF THE BRAIN AND THREE BASIC LAWS

Based on his extensive neuropsychological research on clinical symptoms resulting from brain damage, Luria (1973a) identified three functional systems, or units, of the brain (as described in Chapter 2). In sum, the first unit is responsible for maintaining cortical arousal and directing attention; the second unit codes information using simultaneous and successive processes; and the third unit is responsible for planning cognitive activities. Luria (1973a, p. 74) also postulated "*three basic laws* governing the work structure of the individual cortical regions comprising the second brain system and which also apply to the next [third] functional unit".

1. The first law involves the hierarchical structure of the second and third functional units. The structures forming the second functional unit (simultaneous and successive processing) are subdivided into (*a*) the primary (projection) areas, which receive corresponding information and analyze it into its elementary components; (*b*) the secondary (projection–association) areas, which are responsible for coding (i.e., synthesizing) these elements and converting somatotopical projections into functional organization; and (*c*) the tertiary areas (or the zones of overlapping), which are responsible for the concerted working of the various analyzers and the production of supramodal (i.e., symbolic) schemes. These schemes form the basis of complex forms of intellectual activity.

The organization of the structures forming the third functional unit is also hierarchical. There is, however, one major difference: in the second functional unit, the "afferent system of the brain, the processes go from the primary to the secondary and tertiary zones; in the third, efferent system, the processes run in a descending direction, starting at the highest levels, the tertiary and secondary zones, where the motor plans and programs are formed, and then passing through the structures of the primary motor area, which sends the prepared motor impulses to the periphery" (Luria, 1973a, pp. 82–83). The tertiary zones of the third functional unit (i.e., the prefrontal area) are highly interconnected with lower levels of the brain and with nearly all other parts of the cortex, as we noticed above. Information that has already been processed in other parts of the cortex is fed through these connections to the prefrontal area. Furthermore, connections with the reticular formation and the autonomic nervous system permit the frontal lobes to assess signals from the organism's internal environment. Thus, the frontal lobes, and particularly the prefrontal area, act as a superstructure above all other parts of the brain, performing a far more universal function of general regulation of behavior than any other part of the brain (Luria, 1973a).

Luria also noticed that the relationship between the three zones changes during the course of human development. In the young child, the proper working of a higher zone depends on the integrity of the lower zones (i.e., the main line of interaction is upward from below). In contrast, in the adult the line of control is from the tertiary zone to the secondary zone and further to the primary zone. Although there are reciprocal connections between the three zones, the sensory projection area is the lowest area and the zones of overlapping (i.e., the tertiary areas) are the highest area.

2. The second law concerns the diminishing modality character of information processing in the three zones. Specifically, the primary zone retains modality characteristics or tags of the information that it receives (i.e., information in this zone is tagged as visual, auditory, tactile, etc.). The modality information diminishes in the secondary zone, which still retains some information about the specific receptor through which the information was received. The secondary zone also has an

integrative role: It synthesizes information that has been received from different sense modalities. The tertiary zone, however, is completely free of modality information and is therefore nonspecific or "supramodal" in character.

It is important that the highest zone be nonspecific in terms of sensory modality because this facilitates the integration of information from all sensory sources. To illustrate this point, imagine what would happen if one could not integrate what one heard in a lecture on a particular topic with what one read about that topic in a book.

3. The third law involves the progressive lateralization of functions within the brain. That is, at the level of the primary zone, there is essentially no difference in the functioning of the left and right hemispheres. At the level of the tertiary zone, however, many functions are lateralized. Speech, for example, is associated with the left hemisphere in the majority of people. The left hemisphere also begins to play an essential role in the cerebral organization of other, higher forms of cognitive activity associated with speech, such as perception organized in logical schemes, logical thought, and active verbal memory (Luria, 1973a). Accordingly, the right hemisphere plays only a subordinate role in the cerebral organization of these processes.

To summarize, Luria described the organization of the various functions of the brain as involving both depth and spread. The three hierarchical levels of primary, sensory-associative or secondary, and tertiary zones imply that there is a certain chain of command in the organization of cognitive functions. On the other hand, the three functional units of the brain and their underlying neurophysiological structures spread over a wide area of the cortical and subcortical regions. Furthermore, these units are interdependent and work in collaboration to produce higher mental activities.

THE FRONTAL LOBES AND PLANNING: RECENT VIEWS

There is a general consensus that many of the functions that are required for planning take place in the prefrontal area (i.e., in the tertiary zones of the frontal lobes). The prefrontal cortex is involved in several cognitive functions and at least three of those functions can be identified as specific to the prefrontal region: provisional short-term memory, preparatory set, and interference control (Fuster, 1989). These three functions operate under the supraordinate function of "temporal organization of behavior".

An important distinction between planning as a functional system and planning as a function must be emphasized (Stuss, 1992). Planning is a frontal system that is intimately connected to the frontal lobes of the brain but the functional entity of a planning task includes operations that involve other areas of the brain. Thus, what occurs in the other parts of the brain is of vital interest if we wish to provide a comprehensive explanation of the neuropsychology of planning. In the remainder of this chapter, however, we will concentrate mainly on the integrative functions of the frontal lobes.

WHAT DO THE FRONTAL LOBES DO?

The influence of the frontal lobes on behavior was largely overlooked in classical neuropsychology since frontal lobe lesions did not seem to produce any specific dysfunctions that could be identified by neuropsychological or intelligence tests (Damasio, 1985). At present, however, most researchers agree that the frontal lobes have an important integrative and control function in behavior and cognitive activity (Stuss & Benson, 1987).

Due to this integrative and controlling role, the frontal lobes are important for a wide variety of cognitive, as well as noncognitive, functions. These include, for example, voluntary attention (Fuster, 1989; Luria, 1973a), target detection and vigilance (Posner & Petersen, 1990), control of both internal and external inference (Fuster, 1989; Pribram, 1973), maintenance of muscle tone and gait (Damasio, 1985), perception, language, and emotions (Stuss & Benson, 1986, 1987), working memory (Fuster, 1989; Goldman-Rakic, 1992), and episodic memory (Squire et al., 1993).

To understand how the frontal lobes can have an effect on such a variety of functions, we need to understand how the brain is organized and how this organization affects behavior and cognitive activities. Our conceptualization of the functional systems is based mainly on the hierarchical model of brain functioning suggested by Stuss and Benson (1986, 1987). Furthermore, it views the hierarchical organization of both functional units (neuroanatomical level) and the functional systems (cognitive level) supported by them as self-evident. Figure 3.2 presents an overview of the hierarchical structure of functional systems and their underlying brain systems (i.e., functional units).

POSTERIOR/BASAL SYSTEMS

The first, hierachically subordinate, level is formed by those functional systems that are hypothesized to be based mainly in the first or

Figure 3.2
Frontal and Posterior/Basal Functional Systems

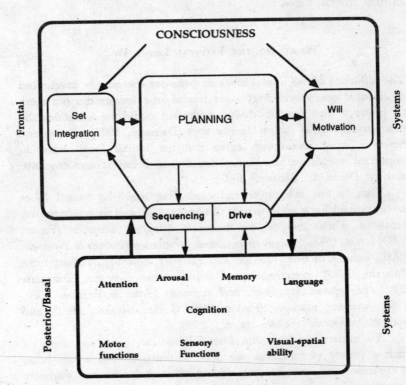

in the second functional unit, as suggested by Luria (1973a). Stuss and Benson (1986, 1987) combine these two units and call these systems "posterior/basal functional systems". According to Stuss and Benson (1986, p. 240), these "systems include a number of recognized neural activities, such as sensory and motor functions, emotion, language, memory, visual–spatial ability, attention, and even general cognitive abilities". Figure 3.2 lists attention, arousal, memory, language, cognition, motor functions, sensory functions, and visual–spatial ability as posterior/basal systems. This list of functions is based on our present knowledge and should therefore be viewed only as a working hypothesis.

Each posterior/basal functional system is reciprocally connected with the prefrontal area (Luria, 1973a), which plays a supervisory, controlling role in their functioning. Stuss and Benson (1986, 1987) suggest, however, that the posterior/basal functional systems can work independently of frontal lobe influence as long as they operate at the level of well-learned and routine functions. Accordingly, the basic activities of these functional systems may not be disturbed by frontal lobe damage. Such damage may, however, cause a dissociation of action from the guiding control of the frontal lobes (Luria, 1973a). When this occurs, the patient, after failing repeatedly to follow instructions and execute correctly a series of actions, can nevertheless verbally reproduce the instructions and his or her intent to carry them out. Furthermore, s/he can fully recognize the errors but fails to correct them or to account for them. Fuster (1989) describes the same phenomenon as resulting from a lesion in the prefrontal area and suggests that it "portends the patient's inability to construct a purposive temporal synthesis incorporating both the plan and the action into a cohesive whole" (p. 162).

In sum, posterior/basal functional systems work under the controlling supervision of the frontal lobes whenever a task requires novel or integrated responses. They work independently of the influence of the frontal lobes whenever the response is well learned and routine.

THREE DIVISIONS OF THE FRONTAL SYSTEMS

The second main block in Figure 3.2 consists of the frontal systems. Stuss and Benson (1986) suggested three separate "divisions" of the frontal systems that are conceptually hierarchical and progressively more abstract. The first level, or division, is formed by sequencing and drive. The second level is formed by executive functions and the third by self-awareness. In the present model, however, executive functions are replaced by planning and self-awareness by consciousness. The reasons for these changes are explained below.

The First Division: Drive and Sequencing

Sequencing refers to the ability to organize separate bits of information into meaningful sequences. *Drive*, in turn, refers to the basic energizing force or need that initiates human motor and mental activity. Decrease in activity or apathy, as well as excessive activity or lack of inhibition, have been linked with frontal dysfunction.

Both sequencing and drive have many of the characteristics of the posterior/basal functional systems but are located in more anterior brain structures: sequencing is likely located in the dorsal–lateral convexity of the frontal lobes and drive is probably situated in the medial sagittal frontal structures (Stuss & Benson, 1986). Like the other two levels of frontal systems, sequencing and drive are superordinate to the posterior/basal systems. Sequencing is particularly important for language functions and for the maintenance of order in motor responses. Drive is closely linked to the first functional unit and its arousal function. Drive differs from arousal, however, in that it has direction and can be controlled by past experiences and learning to a greater extent than arousal.

Formation of sets and *integration* are closely connected to, and partly dependent upon, sequencing (Stuss & Benson, 1986, p. 242). Formation of sets refers to the ability to extract essential data from multiple bits of information and to form related sets of information from this material. Set formation is a key factor in producing new, more complex information from available data. Integration refers to the ability to extract related information from different sets and to integrate it into new knowledge or into an understanding of a complex situation. As indicated in Figure 3.2, we believe that both set formation and integration are more complex mental functions than sequencing. This is mainly due to the fact that both of these functions, and integration in particular, can be under the control of conscious plans. In other words, our plan, with its accompanying goals and objectives, directs the formation of sets and the integration of both new and old knowledge into relevant data matrices. Thus, set formation and integration do not form a separate level of frontal systems but instead, are integrative functions that are dependent on all three divisions of the frontal systems.

In an analogous manner, *will* and *motivation* are reciprocally connected to drive. We believe that drive is more unconscious than motivation or will, although all of them can be controlled by conscious plans, especially by the goals and objectives of plans. Furthermore, will and motivation are more intellectual, and less biological, functions than drive. That is, drive is controlled largely by biological factors and past experiences, whereas will and motivation are controlled more by reflection and anticipated goals and objectives. Thus, like set formation and integration, will and motivation are integrative functions that are dependent on all three divisions of the frontal systems.

The Second Division: Planning

The second division or level of the frontal systems is of most interest to us and we will therefore examine it more closely. Different researchers have named and defined this system in somewhat different (although highly related) ways. But irrespective of the name given to the second division, most researchers have agreed that it is clearly allied with the prefrontal cortex.

Stuss and Benson (1986) suggest that the second division of the frontal systems is formed by executive functions in general and control in particular. They further suggest that control and executive functions are needed in nonroutine, novel situations that require the creation of a new solution and include at least the following functions: anticipation, goal selection, preplanning (i.e., means-end establishment), monitoring, and use of feedback. According to Stuss and Benson (1987, p. 146) behavior in a novel situation can be described with the help of these categories: "First, a goal must be anticipated and established; and then planning is necessary; a series of "means-end" statements evaluates potential outcomes. Once behavior is initiated the action must be carried out in proper order and results of the behavior must be evaluated (if-then) to monitor results".

In his theory of prefrontal functions, Fuster (1989) postulated that the formation of temporal structures of behavior with a unifying purpose or goal—in other words, the structuring of goal-directed behavior—is the higher order function of the prefrontal cortex. He proposed that all behavior can be conceptualized as consisting of hierarchically organized units. The units that are controlled by the prefrontal cortex are higher in the hierarchy and are defined by their purpose or goal rather than by their elementary units. The purposes or goals of these units may vary from biological to intellectual needs, can be unconscious as well as conscious, can be hierarchically organized so that one purpose serves as a step toward another purpose, and always imply a future goal. Moreover, the behavior used to realize a particular purpose is not terminated until the goal is achieved.

Fuster (1989) further suggested that the temporal organization of behavior can be subdivided into three subordinate functions: anticipatory set, provisional memory, and the control of interference. Anticipatory set, or preparation, includes the anticipation of future events in the behavioral structure and the preparation of the organism for them. This prospective function is firmly rooted in the past: "Experience allows the organism to form, out of old elements, the cognitive scheme of the plan that is to serve as the template for new action" (Fuster, 1989, p. 164). Apart from involving a plan or a scheme of action, anticipation includes the preparation of the sensory and motor apparatus for each situation. This is done in order to optimize the reception and employment of incoming information in accordance with the plan. For example, if we need a certain book from the library, our anticipatory set would include building a plan for this procedure as well as preparing for receiving relevant information about the location of the book.

Provisional or short-term memory refers to the temporal representation and retention of the entire scheme of action that guides behavior, as well as to any acts that are part of it. Provisional memory is distinguished by its context and goal rather than by its content. Using the library example, if our goal is to go to the library and find a particular book, provisional memory would integrate old and new information about the title of the book, the route to the library, the catalog system, and so forth. After the book is found, this particular provisional memory is no longer useful and must be discarded in order to make room for new information.

The control of interference, in turn, refers to the prevention of disruptive influences resulting from unrelated external and internal stimuli. On our way to the library, for example, we may encounter an acquaintance who wants us to join her for lunch or if we arrive at the library, we may be overwhelmed by the multitude of other library users and may never locate our book or find the card catalog. These are all external interferences, but we also need to inhibit internal interferences such as impulses to do something else instead or the names of other books that we have read and memorized.

Clearly, our definition of planning (see Chapter 2) includes both what Stuss and Benson (1986) mean by executive functions and what Fuster (1989) means by temporal organization of behavior. The only element of the models presented above that our definition of planning does not deal with is the provisional memory function of the frontal lobes proposed by Fuster. This component is hardly an integral part of planning as a cognitive function, although it is undoubtedly an important condition for planning to occur. Moreover, we feel that our definition of planning captures the active, goal-oriented nature of this process, as well as its multilevel structure, better than either of the above notions. Therefore, we suggest that the second level of frontal systems is planning.

The Third Division: Consciousness

Consciousness (i.e., self-consciousness, self-awareness, self-reflectiveness) is necessary for planning, that is, for the regulation and control of activity in accordance with one's goals. The frontal lobes, particularly the prefrontal cortex, are essential for functions that the term consciousness refers to and which are considered the highest and most "human" of all mental abilities. Patients with frontal lobe lesions, for example, often display diminished self-consciousness and, accordingly, fail to regulate their activity in a meaningful manner (Luria, 1973a).

Consciousness is a difficult topic for cognitive psychologists and neuropsychologists interested in planning. On the one hand discussions of consciousness exist in many philosophical systems; these cannot, however, be easily connected with psychological investigations. William James, a noted philosopher and psychologist, distinguished between consciousness that is apparent to the individual and various other forms of consciousness that lie beyond it. He maintained that normal waking consciousness, the rational one with which we are familiar, is just one type of consciousness and that other, entirely different, varieties also exist (James, 1958). Indeed, the cognitive processes involved in planning or in arriving at a clinical judgement are not at all apparent. Broadbent, Fitzgerald and Broadbent (1986) have shown that when too many factors are involved in planning or decision making, individuals become unaware of the underlying cognitive processes that shape their decisions. This means, for example, that the notion of metacognition, a popular explanatory construct in current psychology, is not entirely representative of these underlying processes because it is "rational consciousness".

Neuropsychologists, such as Luria, who study various forms of aphasia, are forced to deal with consciousness and its relationship to language. This is discussed further by Luria (1973a, pp. 93–94), who clearly states the role of speech not only in the formation of conscious activity but also in its control:

> The chief distinguishing feature of the regulation of human conscious activity is that this regulation takes place with the close participation of *speech*. Whereas the relatively elementary forms of regulation of organic processes and even of the simplest forms of behaviour can take place without the aid of speech, *higher mental processes are formed and take place on the basis of speech activity*, which is expanded in the early stages of development, but later becomes increasingly contracted. . . . It is therefore natural to seek the programming, regulating and verifying action of the human brain primarily in those forms of conscious activity whose regulation takes place through the intimate participation of speech.

The above quotation describes the roles of inner and external speech in planning. But not all planning is conscious and in many "lower level" planning tasks, such as Visual Search, the search strategy may be automatic because it has been well rehearsed and has become a habitual behavior.

Undoubtedly, we still lack the tools to study consciousness as the culmination of all mental activities. Ornstein's (1972) complaint in this regard, as expressed in *The Psychology of Consciousness* is still valid. However, urging psychologists to tackle intractable Eastern ideas of consciousness, such as the stage at which the difference between subject and object disappears, only makes the task more difficult.

COMPONENTS OF PLANNING

Figure 3.3 identifies five components of planning: goals and objectives, anticipation, representation, execution, and regulation. These components are meant to summarize the definition of planning provided in Chapter 2. The generation and selection of goals and objectives is an integral part of planning activity. All planning is guided by a goal or purpose, although the objective may not be readily available to the planner, as discussed in Chapter 2.

Figure 3.3
Planning as a Frontal System

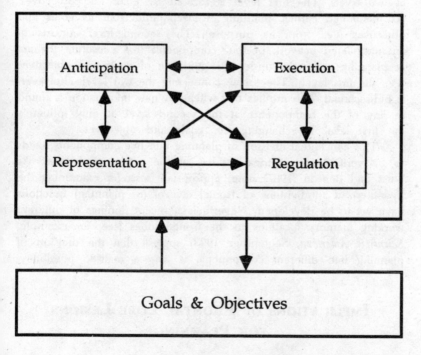

Anticipation includes the ability to predict the consequences of a plan or a behavior, the selection and shaping of environments in order to reach favorable consequences, and the selection of subgoals. We also anticipate future actions and prepare for them in several ways (Fuster, 1989).

Representation involves several activities: making plans, considering conditions for their application, and setting up subgoals when the ultimate goal is too distant and requires a complex set of activities. It includes both the original plan of action and a dynamic sequence of alternative activities.

Execution can consist of planning-in-action or carrying out an advance plan of action. Finally, regulation refers to the monitoring and controlling of behavior according to the plan and revising the plan when necessary.

Thus, in Figure 3.3, the components of planning are represented at two levels. The first level is formed by goals and objectives. As mentioned earlier, planning is inseparable from its goals and objectives (i.e., from its purpose). The second level consists of an interrelated network of four components that constitute the act of planning and work under the guidance of goals and objectives (i.e., the first level). The arrow connecting the two levels, however, is bidirectional. This implies that whenever new information is found in any of the components at the second level, it may influence the first level by changing the goals and objectives.

This conceptual division of planning into five components needs to be verified in empirical studies at the neurological level. As Stuss and Benson (1987) note, appropriate tests for examining the hypothesized subdivisions of frontal control (or planning) functions have yet to be developed. Nevertheless, recent findings of different working memory locations in the frontal lobes (see, for example, *Scientific American*, September 1993) suggest that the division of planning into different components is also a realistic possibility.

IMPLICATIONS OF FRONTAL LOBE LESIONS FOR PLANNING

Frontal lobe lesions can cause a number of dysfunctions, both cognitive and noncognitive. For example, motor functions and attention can be disturbed; self-awareness, personality and emotions can be abnormal; and sensory–perceptual functions, visual–spatial functions, speech and language, memory, cognition, and executive system functions can be damaged (Stuss and Benson, 1986). Fuster (1989) identified the following disorders as "prefrontal syndromes": disorders of attention and perception (for example, lowering of general awareness, sensory neglect, distractability, disorders of visual search and gaze control, difficulty in concentration); disorders of motility (for example, hypokinesis, hyperkinesis); disorders of temporal integration (for example, defective memory, defective planning, defective control of interference); and disorders of affect and emotion.

But the precise diagnosis of dysfunctions is not an easy matter. At present, frontal functions can be examined only through the medium of other functions such as posterior/basal functions (Stuss & Benson, 1987). One approach involves constructing tests that can separate the superordinate frontal control (or planning) functions from the more basic posterior/basal functions like simultaneous and successive processing, or attention and arousal. This, however, creates a problem: a lesion in the posterior/basal areas can manifest in some planning functions but not in others. Thus, diagnosing frontal lobe dysfunctions must always rely on several tests that involve different posterior/basal systems.

There is yet another difficulty in diagnosing frontal lobe lesions using neuropsychological tests. In terms of the relationship between brain and cognitive functions, the classical localization theory assumes that the probability of a particular neuropsychological syndrome is determined solely by the neuroanatomic site of the lesion. Goldberg and Bilder (1987), however, argue that there are several reasons to believe that the frontal lobes, and particularly the prefrontal cortex, do not fit this assumption of isomorphism. Instead, the prefrontal cortex is functionally more vulnerable and more likely to "mirror" disturbances affecting different loci in the brain than any other brain structure. There are at least three different reasons for this. First, the prefrontal area has uniquely rich connections to other functional systems of the brain, both cortical and subcortical, and affects and receives impulses from these systems. Second, prefrontal cortex is among the youngest cortical areas phylogenetically, as well as the slowest to develop ontogenetically. According to a "Jacksonian" conceptualization of evolution and dissolution, both of these facts would make the prefrontal cortex more vulnerable to disruption (Goldberg & Bilder, 1987). Finally, if there is generalized structural damage to the brain, it is likely to affect the least overlearned and least routinized behaviors the most. The functions of the prefrontal cortex are more complex than those of any other cerebral region and are therefore more likely to manifest problems.

What all of this means is that a "frontal syndrome", or the breakdown of control functions usually associated with a frontal lobe lesion, can be produced by a diffuse brain dysfunction affecting much of the brain, as well as by a specific frontal lobe lesion (Goldberg & Bilder, 1987). Thus, the description of frontal lobe pathology is not necessarily accompanied by the specification of the respective lesioned areas. Terms such as "executive control function" (Lezak, 1983; Stuss & Benson, 1986), "supervisory system" (Shallice, 1988), or "planning" relate more directly to a cognitive level of analysis and are sometimes used without reference to underlying anatomical disturbances (Stuss, 1992).

After these cautionary notes we should remind the reader that several researchers have written directly about the effects of frontal lobe lesions on problem solving and planning. The next section briefly presents the most common findings of these studies.

FINDINGS FROM EMPIRICAL STUDIES

Luria and Tsvetkova (1990) and Luria (1973a) viewed problem solving as the most definite and complete manifestation of intellectual activity (i.e., thinking). Therefore, the neuropsychological analysis of problem solving and its impairment after cortical lesions would generate information not only about the localization of different functional systems but also about thinking and the structure of intellectual activity in general. As a consequence, Luria invested a great deal of time in identifying the specific cognitive deficiencies exhibited by patients with different cortical lesions. Due to the central role that the frontal lobes play in Luria's conceptualization of functional units, he was specifically interested in the consequences of lesions to this area of the brain.

Patients with frontal lobe lesions suffer primarily from a pronounced change in the structure of their mental activity. Luria and Tsvetkova (1990) offered the following summary of these patients' cognitive functioning:

1. Frontal lobe patients do not analyze the meaning of a statement of a given problem; they do not attempt to distinguish essential information or compare different components of a statement.
2. They do not develop a plan or program for solving a problem that would proceed from a preliminary analysis of the stated information. Instead, their attempts to solve a problem are impulsive, that is, their answers are based on fragments of information that, for some reason, have attracted their attention.
3. They find it difficult to shift from one operation to another and exhibit perseveration and a lack of flexibility.
4. They do not evaluate their responses against the original information or do not determine whether the outcome agrees or disagrees with the original intention.

In sum, Luria and Tsvetkova (1990) describe cognitive activity that is very uncontrolled in character. These observations were originally reported some 30 years ago. It is heartening to see more recent support for Luria's findings (see, for example, Fuster, 1989; Hecaen & Albert, 1978; Perecman, 1987; Shallice, 1988; Stuss & Benson, 1984, 1986). Also, several recent formulations of the role of the frontal lobes in problem solving have been based on Luria's work (see, for example, Damasio, 1985; Stuss & Benson, 1986).

One recent review (McCarthy & Warrington, 1990) identified well over 20 studies that had found problem solving difficulties in patients with frontal lobe lesions. These difficulties manifested in one or more of the following functions: formulation of strategies, anticipatory processes, flexibility, and evaluation of performance. The authors also noticed, however, that localization or lateralization of these functions within the frontal lobes had not been very successful. They concluded that the tasks that have been used are often complex and thus involve multiple processing systems.

Luria, of course, realized that experimental and clinical studies have only just begun to unravel the complex functions associated with the frontal lobes. Although a great deal of progress has been made, there is still a sense of mystery surrounding the frontal lobes (Stuss & Benson, 1986). We still have very little definite knowledge about the overall functioning of the frontal lobes and different researchers seem to emphasize different facets of its functions as the core of "frontal syndrome" or deny altogether the existence of a single "frontal syndrome" (see e.g., Damasio, 1985). Several studies, however, have produced comparable results. The following is a brief account of the most common findings as summarized by Stuss and Benson (1986) and Fuster (1989):

1. The first finding relates to the dissociation between action and knowledge, and action and speech. Luria (1973a) considered language and speech to be the central mechanisms for regulating human activity. Stuss and Benson (1986) proposed that frontal lobe damage can result in impaired verbal control of behavior. Specifically, frontal lobe patients may verbalize a task correctly but fail to use this information to direct their behavior. Thus, intact verbal knowledge and description of actions are dissociated from performance.

2. A second finding is concerned with sequential behaviors. Again, Luria emphasizes the importance of the frontal lobes for carrying out actions in an instructed sequence, where the instruction could arise from an external or an internal source. Fuster (1989) suggested that disorders involving the temporal integration of behavior are the most common consequence of prefrontal damage. These disorders manifest most commonly as an inability to initiate and carry out novel action sequences for reaching goals. Moreover, difficulties in dealing with novel situations result in a lack of flexibility. For instance, any task that requires a frequent change of strategies would be performed poorly by patients with frontal lobe damage. Frontal lobe damage is associated with impaired ability to both form and alter a set.

3. Lack of inhibitory control is a related disorder apparent after prefrontal damage. Such damage impairs the ability to maintain a set in the face of interference from both internal and external sources (Fuster, 1989). When the suppression of inappropriate and untimely responses is deficient, the patient can manifest disorganized cognitive activity as well as disorganized patterns of behavior.

4. Frontal lobe damage can lead to reduced motivation and initiation of behavior, as well as reduced self-awareness. Thus, patients with frontal lobe damage may display problems in both the activation and inhibition of behavior. For example, disorders of general motor activity are frequent after frontal lobe insult and range from a hyperactive to a hyperkinetic state (Stuss

& Benson, 1986). Also, prefrontal damage can impair the ability to monitor personal behavior. Thus, patients with prefrontal lesion may not be able to use feedback in tasks such as sorting.

In sum, disorders of initiating, controlling, monitoring, and regulating behavior on the basis of feedback appear to be frequent after frontal lobe damage, suggesting that the frontal lobe is the center for planning behavioral and cognitive activity. Planning has, however, frequently been assessed as a general frontal lobe function. The neuropsychological literature has only infrequently considered the heterogeneity and diversity of symptoms that can arise from frontal lobe damage and their specific location within the frontal lobes. Furthermore, very few neurophysiological or cognitive theories have led to the construction of specific frontal lobe tests. Given all this, the frontal lobes remain an uncharted frontier.

4

THE DEVELOPMENT OF PLANNING

The study of the development of planning skills was neglected by psychologists long after planning had become a central concept in general cognitive psychology. Even today, there is virtually no theoretical work in this area and the major sources of data concerning children's planning skills and their development are studies involving other cognitive functions (for example, children's memory). These studies deal mainly with the execution of previously learned plans and not with the actual process of generating plans and implementing them in new situations (Kreitler and Kreitler, 1987). Studies on children's problem-solving behavior, in turn, have often focused on identifying aspects of cognition that characterize failure to attain successful problem outcomes (i.e., identifying what children are unable to do). The results of these studies have indicated that children: (a) have difficulties processing and organizing sets of cognitive subprocesses, and retaining relevant stimulus information; (b) have difficulties attending and shifting attention to relevant stimulus aspects; (c) become frustrated and perseverate more easily; (d) lack motivation and logical abilities; and (e) are unable to make use of feedback (see Parrill-Burnstein, 1978). Comparing children's problem-solving performances with those of adults clearly gives us an exceedingly negative picture of children's cognitive skills and provides little information about the gradual development of planning abilities.

There are two areas of research that have produced data, often indirectly, about the development of planning skills. One is the vast field of developmental psychology which has, since the time of Piaget and Vygotsky, shown a special interest in the development of children's intellectual skills and produced, as a byproduct, studies focusing on planning skills in particular. Developmental psychologists have, however, approached the development of planning skills in a variety of ways, with the result that there is presently little consensus in the field. Here, as in cognitive psychology, different researchers have defined planning in different (and sometimes conflicting) ways and the behaviors that they have interpreted as planful have also varied accordingly.

There are three major approaches within developmental psychology for researching children's planning skills. The first approach equates the term planful with deliberate means-end behavior. According to this approach, rudimentary means-end behaviors such as removing a barrier in order to retrieve an object, which is evident during the sensorimotor stage of human development (Piaget, 1963), would qualify as planned actions.

In the second approach, the target of analysis is also planful behavior but the presence of planful behavior alone is not a sufficient condition for inferring the existence of planning. The researcher must also show that the child formed a mental representation (i.e., a plan) of the series of actions before undertaking them. This approach is based on a conceptualization of planning similar to that of Hayes-Roth and Hayes-Roth (1979) discussed in Chapter 1.

The third approach focuses on plan formation. In a typical plan formation study, the subject has to construct a plan for solving a hypothetical problem (for example, running errands or playing a game) without an intention to implement the plan. This plan, or the process leading to it that the researcher has recorded, is then analyzed rather than analyzing the subject's behavior on a practical task (as occurs in the second approach). Often subjects are asked to think aloud while planning. The third approach has two obvious strengths. First, it avoids the problem of misdiagnosis: the target of analysis is an explicated plan produced by the subject in a new and hypothetical situation or a verbal protocol produced by the subject while formulating the plan. Thus, planning as a mental process is necessarily present. Second, this approach can be used to analyze the "microgenesis" of a plan, that is, how a plan may develop within a planning session as a result of recurrent revisions. The disadvantage of this approach is that it often requires subjects to possess advanced linguistic skills in order to be capable of communicating their intentions to the researcher. Moreover, it requires that subjects have sufficient intrinsic motivation to adopt a planning approach in a hypothetical situation that may have little relevance to their everyday lives. These requirements make the plan-formation approach unsuitable for studying the early developmental stages of planning.

The second area of research that has produced relevant data on the development of planning is the emerging field of developmental neuropsychology, an area of study focusing on the relationship between cognitive functions and the developing brain. As was noted in Chapter 3, planning is a frontal lobe function. But the frontal lobes are important for a wide variety of other cognitive (as well as noncognitive) functions aside from planning. This diversity of responsibilities assigned to the frontal lobes may be responsible for the diversity of opinions about their functional (as opposed to biological) maturation.

Luria (1973a) suggested that the prefrontal areas of the cortex involved in planning do not mature functionally until ages 4 to 7. Alternatively, Golden (1981) argued that the prefrontal areas are essentially nonfunctional prior to adolescence. Both of these views imply that the functional development of the frontal lobes is an "all-or-nothing" process and that they are nonfunctional up to a certain age, followed by a transition period during which they mature and begin to assume their role in cognitive functioning. Accordingly, planning as a mental activity is not possible before the transition period. Researchers sharing this view usually concur with Luria and argue that the transition period takes place during the preschool years.

The existence of a specific transition period has been questioned by several researchers. Welsh and Pennington (1988) suggest that these views are based mainly on studies using measures that have proved sensitive to frontal lobe dysfunction in adults but which have not been designed with children's different developmental levels in mind. They argue in favor of adopting the cognitive construct of "executive functions" as a general descriptor of behaviors reflecting frontal lobe activity. They define executive functions "as the ability to maintain an appropriate problem-solving set for attainment of a future goal" (p. 201). This can involve one or more of the following: (*a*) an intention to inhibit a response or to defer it to a later, more appropriate, time; (*b*) a strategic plan of action sequences; and (*c*) a mental representation of the task, including the relevant stimulus encoded in memory and the desired future goal state. Welsh and Pennington add that the advantage of representing the functioning of a brain system by a broad cognitive construct like executive functions is that the entire continuum of behavioral responses across development can then be observed more readily. In other words, if only highly organized strategies were included in our definition of frontal lobe functions, we would overlook behaviors reflecting goal directedness, planning, and set maintenance, which are already evident during the first three years of development. Welsh and Pennington maintain that by using the above-mentioned definition of executive functions, elementary forms of frontal lobe functioning can be observed early in ontogenesis and have a prolonged course of development—more protracted than, for example, the developmental course of handedness or many aspects of language. A cautionary note, however, is in order: if we are to study the development of planning as defined in Chapter 2, it is hardly appropriate to infer the existence of planning ability after witnessing one or two of its components. Thus, the presence of a future orientation or inhibition alone is not sufficient to determine that a child is capable of planning his or her activity (or even his or her operations).

We will now review some of the literature in both developmental psychology and neuropsychology that has produced data relevant to planning. Note that in the discussion that follows the term planning is used rather loosely and in ways that sometimes do not agree with our earlier definition of it. Also, the cross-sectional nature of some of the studies described makes the age divisions in our subtitles somewhat arbitrary.

PLANNING AND EXECUTIVE FUNCTIONS IN INFANCY

Studies focusing on the earliest forms of planned action in human infants have often equated planning with simple means-end behavior. If we understand planned action as deliberate means-end behavior, it is present early in development. According to Piaget (1963), this form of behavior can already be found in Stage IV of the sensorimotor period (i.e., at approximately 9 months of age) when infants learn to remove a cover from a container in order to get at the object inside. In a typical Stage IV object permanence task, the infant watches as the experimenter hides a toy under one of the two identical cups or in one of the two identical wells, which are then covered. After a brief delay (2 to 10 seconds), the infant is allowed to search for the toy and usually reaches for the correct cup or well. When the toy is transferred to the other cup or well, however, the infant typically continues to reach for the previous location even though the change was performed in her or his full view. Piaget (1963) believed that successful completion of this task signalled the emergence of intelligent behavior because the task requires intentionality toward outside goals and foresight in that at least one intermediate act must be executed before the goal is reached.

While the presence of planning in classical object permanence tasks can be questioned, some researchers have used versions of the task that deal more directly with planning. The best example of this is a study by Willatts (1984). His main interest was young (9 months of age) children's notion of support and their ability to exploit support relations in order to solve a simple problem. The problem confronting the infant involved retrieving a visible but out of reach object (a toy) by first removing a barrier and then pulling a support (a piece of cloth) on which the toy rested. The barrier was introduced in order to control infants' natural tendency to hold something but at the same time, Willatts created a task in which infants had to complete two separate acts (i.e., remove the barrier and pull the support) in order to obtain the toy. The control situation was otherwise similar but the toy was placed beside the cloth and the infant therefore had no means of obtaining it. Willatts' results showed that infants in the experimental group reached for, removed the barrier, and then pulled the cloth in order to get the toy. Infants in the control group stopped to play with the barrier significantly more often than infants in the experimental group. The experimental group was also significantly faster than the control group, making contact with the toy long before the control group had even touched the cloth. In addition, the experimental group made contact with the cloth in almost every trial while the control group made contact with the cloth significantly less often.

Willatts (1984) suggested that infants were able to use a strategy of means-end analysis for solving this problem. He argued further that if infants had been using a simple forward-search strategy, the two groups should not have shown differences in the first action on the barrier. In any case, his results indicate the existence of early abilities for planning a course of action. Neuropsychological studies using similar definitions of planning and subjects of the same age have also produced equivalent results and are discussed below.

Diamond and Goldman-Rakic have attempted to link the executive functions in infants to frontal lobe functioning by combining results from human and animal studies (see, e.g., Diamond & Goldman-Rakic, 1983, 1985, 1986, 1989). This line of inquiry has included (a) studying the developmental progression of human infants and infant rhesus monkeys on tasks assumed to depend on frontal lobe functioning and (b) determining the neural basis of these tasks directly through studies of brain functioning in operated and unoperated adult and infant rhesus monkeys. Using both adult and infant animals is essential in order to control for the possibility that different neural systems may underlie successful task performance at different ages (Diamond, 1991).

Diamond and Goldman-Rakic (1983, 1989) administered the object permanence task to infants between 7.5 and 12 months of age and to intact and operated adult rhesus monkeys with either bilateral prefrontal lesions or bilateral parietal lesions. The results indicated that 7.5- to 9-month-old infants did not succeed in this task and performed similarly to monkeys with bilateral frontal lesions. At 12 months of age, infants could find the object even after a delay of 10 seconds. Unoperated and parietally operated monkeys performed similarly to the older infants. Diamond, Zola-Morgan, and Squire (1989) repeated the latter findings by using unoperated and hippocampally (traditionally thought to be important for memory and spatial functions) operated adult monkeys. According to Diamond and Goldman-Rakic (1989), these findings suggest that in monkeys, performance on the object permanence task depends upon dorsolateral prefrontal cortex and that the early maturation of the corresponding area in human infants may underlie their reported developmental improvements in object permanence.

Diamond and Goldman-Rakic (1986) and Diamond (1991) replicated these results by using two different tasks (delayed response and object retrieval) with both adult and infant monkeys. The delayed response task differs from the object permanence task only in the schedule for determining where the desired object is to be hidden. In the delayed response task the object is hidden randomly according to a predetermined pattern. The object retrieval task was designed to tap the ability to relate information spanned over space, as well as the ability to inhibit inappropriate motor responses. In this task, the infant tries to retrieve a toy that is placed inside a clear Plexiglas box. Only one side of the box is open and in order to retrieve the toy, infants have to inhibit reaching that is based on their line of vision, find the opening, and relate this information to their motor movements.

Diamond and Goldman-Rakic reported that in these tasks, human infants showed similar development to that displayed in the object permanence task. Infant monkeys, who were tested on all three tasks, showed a developmental progression similar to that of human infants and at the age of 4 months they were at the same level of performance as 12-month-old infants. Monkeys which received bilateral lesions of dorsolateral frontal cortex at 4.5 months could no longer perform any of these tasks. Unoperated, parietally operated, and hippocampally operated adult monkeys showed excellent performance on delayed response and object retrieval tasks, whereas the performance of adult monkeys with lesions in dorsolateral prefrontal cortex was significantly impaired (Diamond, 1991; Diamond & Goldman-Rakic, 1986; Diamond et al., 1989).

Improvement associated with the types of tasks mentioned above indicates development of the ability to use recall to guide action and to overcome the tendency to repeat earlier actions. In other words, it indicates the beginnings of the ability to guide action by intention rather than by habit (Diamond, 1985). Rudimentary forms of these abilities are present in animals and develop during the second half of the first year in human infants.

Tasks such as object permanence and delayed response seem to be appropriate for assessing frontal lobe functioning in human infants. For reasons that are not clear (language probably being one), human adults may not show the delayed response deficit associated with prefrontal damage that other primates invariably show (Fuster, 1989). This is an important discrepancy because it indicates that early goal-directed functions are essentially different from later planning processes. We would like to call the early stage of frontal lobe functioning the preverbal, preplanning stage. It can be argued that the "planning" measured in the above-mentioned tasks is strictly practical and implicit in the task and the context, and therefore more a property of a particular task and context than of a subject. Moreover, it is preverbal in nature and, in Vygotskian terms, belongs to the sphere of prelinguistic intelligence. While the abilities present in this stage relate more closely to simultaneous processing and attention skills (see Chapter 1) than to planning, they can be seen as the first variables in the "genetic–experimental" (Vygotsky, 1978) analysis of planning development. Intentionality and recall in guiding action are both necessary conditions for the later development of complex verbal planning processes.

PLANNING IN EARLY CHILDHOOD

When studying planned actions, a researcher can make invalid inferences about subjects' internal processes when observing their behavior. The goal-directed behavior of young children may appear planful to a researcher even though the child may reach the same result by using alternative methods such as direct search, sighting, or learning over trials. Ruling out these nonplanful alternatives is a difficult problem and few studies have succeeded in doing this with young children (Wellman, Fabricius, & Sophian, 1985).

Wellman and his colleagues (Wellman et al., 1985; Sophian & Wellman, 1987; Wellman, Somerville, Revelle, Haake, & Sophian, 1984) have tried to solve diagnostic problems involved in studying planned actions by developing experimental designs where other, nonplanful, approaches to the task can be controlled for. In a typical search task used by Wellman and his colleagues, children must search all of a number of locations in order to find an object (or objects) hidden in them. The possible planfulness of their search is then determined by examining the route they chose to travel, especially whether they planned their route beforehand so as to minimize the distance to be travelled. By manipulating designs, Wellman and his colleagues have tried to distinguish between planned search and alternative methods that they refer to as "sighting". In planned search, the child forms a representation of the route beforehand and aims at minimizing the distance, whereas in sighting, the child proceeds step-by-step according to which step "looks good" at each successive point. Wellman et al. (1985) believe that sighting is a problem-solving approach that develops earlier than planning because it requires less "future" orientation as well as a less comprehensive consideration of different alternatives.

Wellman et al. (1985) report on two experiments in which they attempted to distinguish between planning and different forms of sighting. In the first experiment, five different search arrays were designed so that different assumed sighting approaches ("line of vision", "proximity", "marker" cue) would conflict with the planning approach. The results indicated that subjects (3-, 4-, and 5-year-old children) clearly preferred sighting: 66 percent of all first searches were based on "line of vision" sighting. Planning was, however, more evident in the children's second searches. If a child chose the middle location (which was on the line of vision) first, s/he still faced a two-location search problem: one of the locations to her/his right and the other to the left. When facing this problem, 51 percent of the 3-year-olds, 69 percent of the 4-year-olds, and 77 percent of the 5-year-olds chose the shortest route, a result that the authors believed to indicate the development of planning. Following the initial hypothesizing set forth by Wellman et al., however, the same results can also be interpreted as suggesting that the second choice was based on a different sighting approach (i.e., avoiding the endpoint marker) when the sighting approach used in the first choice was no longer useful. Wellman et al. do not discuss this possibility but instead, summarize the results in two points: first, sighting seems to play a strong and early role in the search behavior of preschool children; and second, planning ability is nevertheless prevalent and grows in dominance during the preschool period.

The main focus of Wellman et al.'s (1985) second experiment was the relative developmental histories of sighting and planning. The results indicated that (a) 3-year-old children's behavior was not planful and that different cues in search arrays affected their searches only minimally; (b) 3.5-year-old children's behavior was influenced more by different arrays and both planning and sighting tendencies seemed to affect their behavior; (c) 4.5-year-old children still showed a pattern of behavior whereby planning and sighting both had a strong impact on their search decisions; and (d) 5.5-year-old children showed essentially more planning behavior than sighting. It is important to emphasize, however, that Wellman et al. used only two search locations (neither of them in the line of vision at the start) in this study, which leaves their results open to competing interpretations. For example, one can suggest that with increasing age, children are better at understanding the importance of avoiding the endpoint. In three out of the four arrays used by Wellman et al. in this study, avoiding the endpoint would have led to search that appeared planful. This approach, however, does not require the child to determine the sequence of actions more than one step at a time.

The experiments and conclusions presented by Wellman et al. (1985) are informative. They clearly exhibit that planning, especially in its early stages, is greatly influenced by context. Different experimental tasks and designs can have a dramatic impact on the results and conclusions of studies of children's planning skills. This can also be demonstrated by comparing the above results with those of Piaget (1976). He assessed 5- and 6-year-old children's problem-solving skills with a relatively abstract task (i.e., the Tower of Hanoi problem) and concluded that 5-year-old children cannot solve a three-disc problem (including 7 moves) even after trial and error. Also, according to Piaget, none of his subjects made a plan or even understood how they would move the tower from one peg to another. The differences in the conclusions presented by Piaget on one hand, and Wellman et al. on the other, suggest that determining the early stages of planning development is a more complicated task than would at first appear. Early planning may be greatly dependent upon several confounding variables such as the abstractness or the various cognitive requirements of the task. A subject's age does not provide sufficient information to predict the presence or absence of planning behavior in different situations.

In studies of *plan formation* the focus of analysis is "the processes and products that emerge when children construct a plan" (Pea & Hawkins, 1987, p. 274). This approach requires that the researcher reliably record the internal plan formation process of the subject. Most often this is done by asking subjects to think aloud while they construct a plan or to communicate their intentions to the experimenter or a peer. This method assumes that all subjects have sufficiently sophisticated linguistic skills, thereby making it difficult to use with preschool children. An example of the use of verbal protocols to study plan formation is provided in Chapter 6.

Klahr and Robinson (1981) used this approach in their study of preschool-aged children's planning and problem-solving behavior. They used a modified version of the Tower of Hanoi task that varied in difficulty and had two different goal states: tower (all objects on one peg) and flat (all pegs occupied). Instead of allowing their subjects (4-, 5-, and 6-year-old children) to make the necessary moves, Klahr and Robinson showed them a model of the desired goal state and one of the initial state, and then asked the children to present a verbal plan for the entire sequence of moves needed to reach the goal state. The results showed that in the tower-ending problems, almost half of the 4-year-olds were able to solve three-move problems; over two-thirds of the 5-year-olds and almost all of the 6-year-olds were able to generate a perfect plan up to four moves; and over half of the 6-year-olds were able to produce a perfect plan up to six moves. In flat-ending problems, however, all groups scored substantially lower than in tower-ending problems but the effect of age was still significant.

While these results reflect the contextual dependence indicated earlier, they also contradict Piaget's (1976) conclusions regarding children's planning skills. By using a modified task and verbal protocols as a target of analysis, Klahr and Robinson (1981) were able to identify planfulness rather than the nonconstructive trial and error behavior observed by Piaget. Klahr and Robinson also made their task more approachable for young children by using a cover story about monkeys (i.e., large daddy, medium-size mommy, and small baby) to explain the differently sized objects. The changes in task and procedure probably helped the authors to use the plan formation approach successfully with preschool children. It is also possible that by asking for a verbal plan of action and preventing their subjects from manipulating the objects, Klahr and Robinson created a condition that "forced" subjects to consider the problem at a more abstract level, thereby resulting in a planful, though incomplete, description of the necessary moves. Perhaps preschool-age children do not easily perceive experimental tasks as requiring planning. Nevertheless, they seem to be capable of employing a planful approach when the context encourages them to do so.

PLANNING AND EXECUTIVE PROCESSES IN LATER CHILDHOOD

Plan formation studies are more commonly used with school-age and adult subjects. Pea and Hawkins' (1987) study is a good example of a plan formation study with school-age children and a developmental focus. Pea and Hawkins wanted to examine the development of planning skills in two different ways: (a) by comparing the planning skills of two different age groups (8- to 9-year-olds versus 11- to 12-year-olds) and (b) by following the "microgenesis" of an individual plan within a planning session. Pea and Hawkins gave their subjects a map of a classroom and asked them to schedule several classroom chores. Subjects were asked to think aloud and to move a pointer to describe the course of their plan. They were given an unlimited amount of time to complete the task and encouraged to try different kinds of plans.

The results of the study indicated that older children were more flexible and efficient planners than younger children. In addition, the efficiency of plans increased from the first to the last plan for both groups. The qualitative analysis of planning protocols showed that the elaboration of subjects' task representations resulted in revisions of the structure of plans: subjects learned to organize chore acts (moves) into clusters more efficiently and to identify identical chore act sequences that could be organized according to the same strategy. This indicates that children engaged in complex, revisionary processes over the course of a single planning session. Also, children's performance with respect to the effectiveness of the plans produced, improved during these revisionary processes.

It should be noted that the nature of the task and procedures used by Pea and Hawkins (1987) probably enhanced the revisionary nature of children's planning. Nevertheless, their results argue strongly against hierarchical, top-down models of children's planning. In Pea and Hawkins' study, children were essentially "planning in action" instead of "planning the action". Furthermore, both experimental groups were planning; the older children were slightly more experienced and used their knowledge slightly more effectively than the younger children.

Neuropsychological studies concentrating on executive functions in later childhood and adolescence have usually emphasized one or more of the following three questions: is development a continuous or a stage-like process? Are executive functions correlated with general intellectual ability? Is there more than one kind of executive function?

The answer to the first question has usually favored the existence of developmental stages. Passler, Isaac, and Hynd (1985) examined the performance level of 64 children between 6 and 12 years of age on several neuropsychological tasks attributed to frontal lobe functioning. They concluded that the development of behaviors associated with the frontal lobes seems to be a multistage process and that the greatest development, reflected in improved performance, seemed to occur between the ages of 6 and 8.

These findings were essentially confirmed by several researchers (Becker, Isaac, & Hynd, 1987; Levin et al., 1991; Welsh, Pennington, & Groisser, 1991) with potential prefrontal tasks selected from literature in both clinical neuropsychology and developmental psychology. Two of the studies (Becker et al., 1987; Welsh et al., 1991) also indicated that 12-year-old children are still less skilled than adults even in some simple tasks, suggesting that the development of executive functions continues well into adolescence.

In addition, Welsh et al. (1991) found that four executive function tasks were uncorrelated with general cognitive ability (as measured by the Iowa Test of Basic Abilities [ITBA]) and that one task correlated positively and two tasks correlated negatively with the ITBA. According to the authors, their results suggest that "executive function is a domain of cognition in normal human development which is relatively independent of IQ" (Welsh et al., 1991, p. 146).

Welsh et al. also performed a factor analysis that extracted three factors instead of one executive function factor. Levin et al. (1991) also found a similar three-factor solution, further indicating that executive functions cannot be conceived of as forming a unitary structure.

It is interesting to note how studies of executive functions support the findings in EEG studies of developmental spurts (see, for example, Hudspeth & Pribram, 1990; Thatcher, 1991, 1992; Thatcher, Walker, & Giudice, 1987). Passler et al. (1985) and Becker et al. (1987) found that the greatest development for the tasks they used occurred between the ages of 6 and 8. The second significant growth spurt involving the frontal lobes takes place between the ages of 4 and 7, and includes the expansion of anterior to posterior connections. The importance of long-distance connections for planning cannot be overemphasized, given that planning involves the synchronization of many specialized processes that take place in the posterior regions of the brain. This synchronization is often a function of the prefrontal cortex and thus the long-distance connections from anterior to posterior parts of the brain are critical for successful performance, especially for more complex planning tasks. Both developmental and cognitive scientists have recognized that between the ages of 4 and 7, children appear to go through a period of rapid development: they learn to master simple planning tasks (Klahr & Robinson, 1981; Welsh et al., 1991); their behavior becomes increasingly verbally mediated (Luria, 1973a); their perseverative responses are greatly reduced (Becker et al., 1987; Passler et al., 1985); and their working memory capacity increases (Case, 1985).

The third growth spurt found by Thatcher et al. (1987) involved right temporal-frontal connections and occurred between the ages of 8 and 10. Neuropsychological studies indicate that by age 10, children have acquired mastery of both verbal and nonverbal proactive inhibition (Becker et al., 1987; Passler et al., 1985), as well as set maintenance and hypothesis testing (Welsh et al., 1991).

The fourth and fifth growth periods, involving primarily different frontal lobe connections, are of great interest in light of the findings of neuropsychological studies. Several relatively simple tasks proved to be difficult for 12-year-olds to perform at an adult level. This suggests that while the strategies needed for these tasks are available to younger subjects, the speed and fluency of their utilization increases with further development of the frontal lobes. It is tempting to suggest that during late adolescence the focus in these types of tasks shifts from constructing a plan to choosing between several possible plans under the guidance of some general regulating principle. This shift probably concurs with the emergence of formal operations during adolescence.

At this point we wish to change the focus of our review and ask "what is planning development the development of?" (Pea, 1982). Electroencephalogram (EEG) studies suggest that at a neural level, the development of planning means better and increased connections between the frontal lobes and other parts of the brain. Unfortunately, psychologists have been far more vague in their answers.

WHAT IS IT THAT DEVELOPS?

There is as yet no generally accepted model of the developmental components and prerequisites of planning as a cognitive activity (Friedman et al. 1987). Some researchers have tentatively suggested that metacognition, representational skills, or strategies for self-control play an important role in the development of planning skills (Scholnick & Friedman, 1987) but very few of them have conducted experimental studies to evaluate directly the importance of these variables for planning development.

Kreitler and Kreitler (1987) have provided the two most comprehensive studies of planning development aimed specifically at describing its developmental components. In two separate studies, they examined children's conceptions of planning (what the Kreitlers refer to as "metaplanning") and children's actual planning performances. Both studies used four groups of subjects (i.e., 5- to 6-year olds, 7- to 8-year olds, 9- to 10-year olds, and 11- to 12-year olds). The authors assumed that the major cognitive tools for planning are acquired between the ages of 5 and 11. Before age 5, action may not yet be sufficiently controlled to allow for enough experience with planning, whereas after age 11, children already have so many stored plans and programs that planning (i.e., plan formation) is not necessary. Even if planning does exist, it is difficult to distinguish from the simple implementation of readymade programs.

In their first study, Kreitler and Kreitler's (1987) main concern was with children's conceptions of planning. The results indicated that children's ideas about the domains to which planning applies changed notably between the ages of 5 and 11: there was both a steady increase in the number of domains considered deserving of planning and a change in the nature of these domains. Younger children considered planning as applicable primarily to regular daily actions centered mostly on oneself, whereas older children considered planning as applicable to actions performed under special circumstances and for both attaining personal goals and solving social and global problems. When asked about the time span that planning is conceived of as involving, older children included the far future along with the immediate and the near future, whereas younger children mentioned only the latter two time spans. Furthermore, older children viewed planning as an increasingly complex and difficult cognitive activity requiring memory, information gathering, and reflection. They also recognized that both adults and children plan, and they learned to evaluate its importance in relation to the task and the context. Whereas younger children mentioned only positive consequences of planning, the oldest group also mentioned possible negative results (for example, less fun, too much control, etc.). Kreitler and Kreitler suggest that conceptions of planning are related to the gradually increasing interest in mastering both the environment and one's own cognitive processes that is characteristic of children between 5 and 11 years of age.

Kreitler and Kreitler's (1987) second study focused on the development of actual planning skills. They designed 10 planning situations based on children's answers in the first study in order to gather information about (a) general planning skills, which are present in various tasks; and (b) task-specific responses, which they referred to as "the techniques and procedures of planning". They found 10 general planning skills that did not occur with significantly higher or lower frequency in any of the planning situations and that could therefore be considered measures of general planning. The following ten measures were used to assess subjects' general planning skills:

1. Number of alternative plans presented (either spontaneously or in response to direct requests in some planning situations).
2. Number of if–then eventualities considered in the plan.
3. Number of chronological orderings used in describing a plan or in asking for information while planning.
4. Number of different questions asked while planning.
5. Number of items considered or referred to.
6. Number of different domains to which the questions or items refer.
7. Number of "general labels" used in presenting a plan or in asking questions while planning.
8. Mean number of steps included in plans presented as first and major plans.
9. Mean number of steps included in plans presented as alternatives to the major plans.
10. Mean number of steps included in all plans, major and alternative ones (Kreitler & Kreitler, 1987, p. 232).

The results revealed significant differences between the four age groups on all 10 variables. There were, however, three distinct developmental patterns: (*a*) a regular linear pattern (variables 6 and 7); (*b*) a nonlinear pattern that consisted of a uniform increase from 5 to 9 years, followed by a significant decrease from 9 to 11 years (variables 1, 2, and 4); and (*c*) an essentially linear pattern that consisted of a uniform increase from 5 to 9 years, followed by slight nonsignificant fluctuations from 9 to 11 years (variables 3, 5, 8, 9, and 10). Kreitler and Kreitler (1987) interpreted these findings to mean that planning develops both quantitatively and qualitatively. The variables that displayed development after the age of 9 represent higher conceptual units that include the longer lists of lower level steps and tasks that the older subjects explicated only when asked to elaborate their plans. Kreitler and Kreitler argued that using "general labels" and "domains" offered several advantages for older subjects: Their plans became more flexible and adaptable, and due to the greater concentration of information, memory load was decreased. The authors also suggested that "general labels" and "domains" form a "program scheme", that is, an overall strategy or set of rules that determine the elements necessary for attaining a goal in a specific situation.

The development of task-specific responses, however, was more complex than anticipated by Kreitler and Kreitler (1987). They concluded that planning develops simultaneously in various directions:

> vertically, in terms of increased hierarchization, and horizontally, in terms of increased number of links or subplans in the plan; with regard to contents, in terms of the meaning elaboration of the problem; and with regard to structure, in terms of the principles used for integrating the different parts of the plan as well as alternate plans (Kreitler and Kreitler, 1987, p. 254).

Kreitler and Kreitler's studies provide an interesting account of the development of planning. Their first study provided evidence that with increasing age, children come to conceive of planning as a complex cognitive activity that can be used to handle a wide variety of situations more efficiently. At the same time, planning as a cognitive activity develops in a variety of ways: plans and alternate plans become more elaborate and flexible; planners become more aware of contextual constraints and begin to ask more questions about them, and begin to consider various "if–then" eventualities (either overtly or implicitly); and planners begin to organize information more efficiently with the help of higher conceptual units. To summarize, we could say that what develops is (a) an awareness and a knowledge base about planning and (b) cognitive abilities to deal with large amounts of information and hypothetical solutions.

Dreher and Oerter (1987) showed that this development continues into early adulthood. They asked subjects ranging in age from 11 to adulthood to schedule an errand-running task with a time constraint and the possibility of using "cultural tools" (e.g., a bicycle) and delegating some of the tasks to a friend. Dreher and Oerter found that the percentage of plans conforming to the time constraint increased with age and that older planners used the bicycle and delegated tasks more often. These results indicate an increase in both social awareness and the capacity to organize a growing number of separate components into a functional plan. According to Dreher and Oerter, the planner needs to recognize and use the deeper and more complex features of the problem and to form a hierarchy of planning operations in order to be able to produce a functional plan. Hence, at this level, planning has to be guided by some general principle such as cost–benefit analysis or maximum speed rather than by the valence of each component of the task.

Pea (1982) probably described the earlier phases of the same developmental trend. He asked two groups of children (8 to 9, and 11 to 12 years of age) about their views of planning. Both groups mentioned that one plans *to do* something and *how to do* something. The second point is important because it indicates that children in both groups were capable of distinguishing means from ends. The older children also mentioned planning the specific *conditions of doing* something. This indicates a rather elaborate representation of planning situations, including the possibility of shaping and selecting one's environments, components that we described earlier as belonging to higher-level activity-planning. The older children also had a better understanding of when and why they do not have to plan, issues that are often socially determined. Thus, their representations also seemed to include some social constraints.

According to Pea (1982), most of the younger children had a magical theory of planning: one will succeed with a good plan but not otherwise. The older children understood that plans are facilitators rather than guarantors of success: plans can be used to enhance the probability of positive outcomes. Pea's results suggest that older children had developed a larger knowledge base about planning, which allowed them to build better representations of planning situations and to adopt a more reflective approach to the process of planning. He also noticed, however, that only a few children in either group mentioned "metaplanning" principles, usually in the context of deciding over goal priorities. This finding indicates that although the older children's approach was increasingly reflective, their planning was still regulated by the context rather than by general planning principles.

SOCIAL AND CONTEXTUAL INFLUENCES

Goodnow (1987) and Baker-Sennett, Matusov, and Rogoff (1993) are critical of much of the recent planning literature for ignoring social and contextual aspects of planning. They argue that in real life, planning is restricted not only by the planner's limited abilities but also by social and contextual constraints on what is feasible and proper. Planning is not considered socially acceptable in all situations; for example, falling in love is something that is often seen as requiring spontaneity rather than advanced planning. Also, planning frequently takes place in organizations and institutions (for example, companies, universities, families) that set contextual limits on the possible outcomes, as well as provide cultural and cognitive tools for the planning process. Additionally, planning usually involves other people as either co-planners, resource persons, or agents to be maneuvered. These features of real-life planning tasks are seldom present in experimental studies.

The studies described thus far in this chapter have resulted in some anecdotal information about the social nature of planning. Kreitler and Kreitler (1987) and Pea (1982) noticed that 11-year-old children did not regard planning positively in all situations. This could be interpreted as meaning that their knowledge of the social constraints on planning had increased compared to younger subjects. Or perhaps it is an age-specific phenomenon: too much planning spoils the spontaneity characteristic of Western teen culture. Dreher and Oerter's (1987) task involved the possibility of delegating some of the errands to a friend but only the oldest subjects were able to make the best use of this possibility. Does this mean that an understanding of the social aspects of planning develops at a later point in time? Goodnow (1987) remarks that we are in need of information about how people use others as resources to complement their own shortcomings and deficiencies. More fundamentally, we also need more information about the development of planning as a social and contextual activity.

Rogoff, Gauvain, and Gardner (1987) offered a rationale for studies focusing on developmental changes in how different contexts can affect children's planning performance. They suggested that the development of planning skills involves an increase in sensitivity to the characteristics of the problem, its contextual features, and relevant knowledge. It also involves an increase in the skills necessary to construct plans in advance when this is appropriate and alertness to the utility of planning in the first place.

Gardner and Rogoff (1990) examined how sensitivity to contextual factors differs in 4- to 9-year-old children. They asked subjects to solve mazes that varied in the appropriateness of advance or improvisational planning. Their results showed that both the older

(7 to 9.5 years of age) and the younger (4.5 to 7 years of age) children adapted their planning to the task circumstances. Both groups used significantly more advance planning for those mazes for which this was appropriate than for the other mazes, and the use of strategies was highly stable over trials. Older children adapted their planning to the circumstances somewhat better than did the younger children, although the difference was not statistically significant. Gardner and Rogoff assumed that this difference resulted from older children being more skilled in advance planning and using this skill selectively whenever such planning was most profitable. In other words, their planning skills and their understanding of the specific characteristics of the situation were more advanced than those of the younger children.

PEER AND ADULT COLLABORATION

Several researchers have investigated how adult and peer collaborators affect children's planning performance. Gauvain and Rogoff (1989) found that collaboration with peers on a simple route planning task did not lead to an improvement in 9-year-olds' performance. In contrast, dyads of 5-year-olds who shared the responsibility of decision making developed more efficient routes than individual planners of the same age. Furthermore, 5-year-olds from these dyads were more efficient planners during individual posttests than were either the children who had a partner but who did not share decision making or the children who worked alone. The same was also true for 5-year-olds from adult–child dyads in which the adult encouraged and included the child in decision-making.

Kontos (1983) studied the effects of parents' verbal directives on children's planning. Her results from two different experiments showed that when parents were permitted to communicate freely with their child while s/he completed a problem-solving task, they displayed a great amount of metacognitive content in their verbal directives. Also, both mothers and fathers displayed more metacognitive content in their verbal directives when speaking to older children (5 years of age) than when speaking to younger children (3 years of age). This did not, however, seem to enhance children's problem-solving performance compared to groups in which parents were not allowed to direct their children. Specifically, in both conditions, children's performance improved during testing but there were no significant differences between the control and the experimental group. There was, however, a significant difference between the older and the younger children. Kontos concluded that her preschool-aged subjects were learning by doing and that their awareness of the task demands increased as much due to practice as to the metacognitive directives received from parents.

Radziszewska and Rogoff (1988) compared the effects of collaboration with adults and with peers in a relatively complex errand scheduling task. Their first study indicated that adult–child dyads used more sophisticated planning methods than peer dyads. The children (9 to 10 years of age) in adult–child dyads were more involved in task completion and communication of planning strategies was more frequent than in peer dyads. As a result, children from adult–child dyads produced better plans in individual posttests than did target children in peer dyads.

In the second study, Radziszewska and Rogoff (1991) also used a third type of dyad: a dyad with a trained peer. Results from this study indicated that the planning displayed by dyads with a trained peer was as sophisticated as that of child–adult dyads. There was, however, more discussion of strategies and more target child involvement in adult–child dyads, which probably accounts for the better posttest performance of children from adult–child dyads compared to target children from each type of peer dyad. The authors attributed the observed differences in target children's planning performances to their greater guided participation: Adult–child dyads involved guidance in the form of verbalization of optimal planning strategies and thinking aloud about planning decisions, and children in these dyads participated actively in decision making and implementation. Exposure to more skilled planning by trained peers did not have the same positive effect as collaboration with adults. This may have resulted from adults being skilled not only in planning but also in collaboration.

How can we explain these somewhat contradictory results? It seems that the mere presence of an adult or peer collaborator is not a sufficient condition for positive effects to be displayed in children's individual posttest planning performance. Communication between partners and the level of shared responsibility are probably important factors in determining outcome. Children's age and task features may also be important factors. Kontos (1983) used simple puzzles and found that adults' metacognitive directives had no positive influence on 3- or 5-year-old subjects' performance. By using a somewhat more complicated task, Gauvain and Rogoff (1989) were able to identify some positive influences on 5-year-old subjects' performance. They also found that working with same-age peers helped 5-year-olds but not 9-year-olds, suggesting that the task was too easy for the older subjects. It seems that the task should be difficult enough to require abstract planning but not so difficult that partners are unable to reflect and discuss the problem (see also Rogoff, 1991).

Tudge (1989) offers an interesting point of view on this matter. He suggests that the beneficial influences of collaboration may be present only in situations in which the more advanced partner is similar to an expert (i.e., both more knowledgeable and confident). If this condition is not satisfied, regression is as probable an outcome of possible cognitive conflict as is development. This line of reasoning suggests that the greater the expertise of the more advanced partner, the greater the chances that the less advanced partner will advance. Dimant and Bearison (1991), however, found that theoretically relevant interaction between partners was associated with higher posttest scores, whereas having a more knowledgeable partner was not. Furthermore, Radziszewska and Rogoff (1988) identified some adult–child dyads that did not lead to positive development despite the almost perfect planning performance of the adults involved. In these dyads, the adults did not communicate their planning processes to the child. Instead, they either excluded the child altogether from task completion or ordered the child to perform parts of the task without providing explanations for the strategy. Radziszewska and Rogoff (1991) argue that the ability to communicate one's own mental processes is a necessary condition for expertise. And perhaps "sensitive responsiveness" (van der Veer & van IJzendoorn, 1988) is a necessary condition for creating "intersubjectivity" (Rommetveit, 1979) or a shared understanding of the situation that may, in turn, be necessary for the successful teaching of expertise.

SCHOOLING

A sociocultural factor of particular importance in any discussion of cognitive development is, of course, schooling. Can planning be accelerated by schooling? Again, very little is known about this issue. Dreher and Oerter (1987) found that subjects who were studying home economics did better in their planning tasks than would have been expected on the basis of their age. Dreher and Oerter assumed that this group had been exposed to equivalent tasks more often during their education than had other subjects. But is the effect of schooling restricted to practices actually engaged in? Das and Dash (1990) suggest that this is not necessarily the case. They administered two simple planning tasks and several syllogistic reasoning tasks to two groups of schooled children (6 to 8, and 10 to 12 years of age) and to two groups of unschooled (same age groups) children. Their results indicated that schooled children outperformed their unschooled counterparts in planning tasks, whereas in syllogistic reasoning, improvement in performance was associated with age and was not enhanced by schooling. These results can probably be explained by the fact that syllogistic reasoning tasks are commonly present within the oral tradition in rural India, whereas the more formal planning tasks are not familiar to either group.

Tanon (1991) compared the influences of formal education to those of informal education (i.e., 2 to 4 years of training in weaving) on planning skills. She used four groups of subjects: schooled weavers, unschooled weavers, schooled nonweavers, and unschooled nonweavers. Also, two tasks were included, one related to weaving and the other related to subjects' everyday lives. The results showed that schooled weavers generally outperformed other groups in both tasks; unschooled weavers and schooled nonweavers performed at roughly the same level on most variables; and unschooled nonweavers obtained the lowest performance scores on both tasks. According to Tanon, the results suggest that informal education in weaving, which requires planning, fosters planning skills in other familiar tasks to the same extent as formal education. The findings also suggest that planning can be accelerated, at least to some extent, by relevant education, both formal and informal.

The above studies indicate that there are many ways in which contextual cues or social interaction can affect children's performance in planning situations. Furthermore, these effects may change as a function of the task and the age of the child. The use of more complex tasks with clearer descriptions of their cognitive requirements would be needed, however, before any firm conclusions could be drawn about the effects of contextual and social stimuli on planning development. Nevertheless, at this point, we can say with some certainty that schooling has a positive influence on children's planning skills. The extent and generalizability of this influence, however, remains to be clarified by future research.

LANGUAGE, THINKING AND PLANNING

Another major contributor to planning development remains to be discussed: language and speech. In most of what follows, we will use the term speech instead of the term language in order to emphasize the active psychological process or activity of talking and communicating rather than the formal structure that the term language normally connotes (see also Wertsch, 1982). In Chapter 2 we defined planning as a higher cognitive function mediated by some symbolic system, most often by language. Accordingly, the development of planning should be, at least to some extent, related to the concomitant development of language (Parrila, 1995). But to obtain information about the importance of speech for planning development, we need to temporarily assume a somewhat broader approach and include some relevant work discussing the relationship between speech and thinking in general.

According to Vygotsky (1986), thinking and speech have different developmental roots and the moment when they converge is the most significant moment in the course of intellectual development, giving "birth to the purely human forms of practical and abstract intelligence" (Vygotsky, 1978, p. 24). This convergence produces verbal thought, which is not the only form of thought but which was clearly given a central role in Vygotsky's theorizing about intellectual development. For Vygotsky, speech is an important factor in the development of thinking in at least three different ways. First, abstract thoughts are formed with the help of speech, that is, speech is the means by which the individual becomes capable of rising above a sensorimotor level of thinking. In this way speech becomes the tool of thought (Vygotsky, 1986). Second, speech, together with written language, is the means by which children obtain access to the accumulated sociocultural experiences in their environment. Finally, with the help of speech, children gradually gain more control over both their internal and external functioning. That is, they learn to regulate their behavior verbally and internally, and thus break the simple stimulus–response chain. Let us now examine each of these points in greater detail.

LANGUAGE AS A TOOL OF THOUGHT

One of the major points in Vygotsky's writings is the claim that higher mental functions, as well as human activity in general, are mediated by tools. Within the context of thinking and planning, the relevant mediators are different types of signs that Vygotsky referred to as "psychological tools". Psychological tools are "internally oriented, transforming the natural human abilities and skills into higher mental functions" (Kozulin, 1986b, p. xxv). Psychological tools do not consist merely of language or linguistic signs but also include gestures, mnemonic techniques, and decision-making systems. It should be noted, however, that Vygotsky emphasized the relationship between speech and thinking far more than any other forms of mediation. As Wertsch (1991) noticed, Vygotsky, as well as most Western researchers after him, assumed "that verbal mediational means would be used as widely and as often as possible" (p. 30). Consequently, after the initial convergence of thinking and speech in early childhood, a child's intellectual growth is contingent upon her or his mastering the tool of thought, that is, language (Vygotsky, 1986).

This position was essentially shared by Carroll (1964), who identified the following factors as possible determinants of an individual's performance in a problem-solving situation: "(1) the individual's repertoire of relevant concepts, (2) the concepts evoked in the individual by the structure of the problem, and (3) the individual's skill in manipulating the concepts evoked, his strategy of solution, his flexibility in changing his mode of attack, and his ability to perceive the relevance of a concept" (p. 85). According to this position, the possession of necessary concepts may be the determining factor in whether or not an individual can solve a problem. Carroll remarks, however, that these concepts are not always coded linguistically and that many intellectual tasks can be performed successfully without the use of linguistic codes.

Carroll's position is relevant here in suggesting that both natural language and other possible symbolic schemes may play a decisive role in thinking and, accordingly, in planning. But how do natural languages or other symbolic schemes act as tools of thought? That is, what symbols do we use when we think? These questions lead us to discuss inner speech and its formative role in thinking.

The term inner speech is usually used to signify "soundless, mental speech, arising at the instant we think about something, plan or solve problems in our mind, recall books read or conversations heard, read and write silently" (Sokolov, 1972, p. 1). In these instances, inner speech is equated with speech to oneself or concealed verbalization. But inner speech can also be understood in a much wider sense as a symbol scheme of thought that is instrumental in understanding and perceiving the world. In this sense, inner speech is the system that mediates between our private, internal reality and the shared, external reality of the world in which we live.

Most psychologists have, however, made two assumptions about inner speech: Inner speech is "the principal mechanism of thought" (Sokolov, 1972, pp. 263-264) and its roots are in spoken language. If we accept these two perfectly rational assumptions, we have to further assume that the possession of the relevant linguistic knowledge can determine an individual's success in a given problem-solving situation. Relevant linguistic knowledge can determine success either directly, as suggested above by Carroll (1964), or through less powerful semantic graphs or "smart symbols" (McNeill, 1987) (i.e., concepts that imply the relevant features of a particular situation). Thus, the extensiveness of our vocabulary and our understanding of relevant concepts should affect our performance in planning tasks. This assumption, however, needs to be qualified: symbols used to solve a planning task that has very little linguistic content may already be so far removed from their linguistic origins that their verbal communication, and thus the verification of their existence using natural language, may be difficult. Consider mathematics, for example: the symbol system used in mathematics is originally defined with the help of natural language but later takes on "a life of its own" to the extent that a mathematician may have overwhelming difficulties in transforming his solution into words.

Consequently, the role of language in planning should always be considered within the context of task demands. Planning tasks with more verbal content and a structure that presupposes (or at least benefits from) verbal mediation, should be affected by language abilities to a greater extent than planning tasks with less verbal content and, for example, more visual structure. Accordingly, Crack-the-Code, Planned Connections, and Number Matching (see next section) should be affected more by language skills than, for example, Visual Search. Whether these assumptions can be experimentally verified remains to be determined.

PLANNING AND COMMUNICATION

Planning plays an important role in modern industrial society, particularly in work life (Dreher & Oerter, 1987) and learning to plan is an essential part of socialization. Moreover, the plans that we use are often socially constructed and our interaction with others has a formative, as well as a facilitative, function in planning development. Even if we assume that rudimentary plans (for example, in the form of goal-directed behavior) exist prelingually in animals and human infants (and may therefore not be affected by verbal communication), the bulk of planning skills—perhaps most of the ones needed for higher order planning, with which we are primarily interested here—are learned through interaction with other, more capable, planners. More often than not, this interaction occurs with the help of language, which is our most powerful tool of communication. Moreover, we need language in order to achieve intersubjectivity, which probably is a necessary condition for teaching (or learning) planning.

Both Luria (1982) and Vygotsky (1978) emphasized the role of the social environment in the development of cognitive processes. One of the basic premises of their theory is that higher cognitive processes have their origins in the interpersonal relationships that the child enters into in his or her environment. In these relationships, the accumulated knowledge of the environment is transmitted to the child by adults (Luria & Yudovich, 1959). According to this premise, possessing inadequate language skills would lead to insufficient acculturation because of limited access to information, which, in turn, would affect the child's thinking skills. This hypothesis is difficult to address, however, since the pivotal role of language in organizing higher mental processes is another central premise in the theories of Luria and Vygotsky, and the two possible ways that language affects a child's intellectual functioning are, to say the least, difficult to separate.

The best examples of studies that have tried to identify the adverse effects of limited communication on intellectual development are perhaps older studies, reviewed by Shif (1969), of mentally handicapped children. According to Shif, the lag in various aspects of speech development limits mentally handicapped children's contact with those around them and thus inhibits to a considerable extent the growth of their cognitive faculties and the acquisition of information transmitted by words. Shif argued further that mentally handicapped children are especially disadvantaged in school learning because the knowledge that they acquire from books is not sufficiently concrete to result in proper development. According to Shif, reproductive representations, when they are based primarily on language, are clearly impeded in the mentally handicapped children. Texts that are read to mentally handicapped children do not call forth sufficient imagery corresponding to the text material, which is not the case with normal children. This was demonstrated by Zankov (1935, cited in Shif, 1969), who showed that mentally handicapped children were able to identify simple causal relationships between phenomena in inanimate nature when those relationships were associated with their real-life experiences. Nevertheless, the same children had difficulties understanding similar causal relationships when these were presented to them in verbal form.

We suggest that limited communication skills lead to limited experiences of the world, which in turn can slow or hinder the learning of new cognitive skills. These negative effects are probably most pronounced in complex and often verbally regulated skills like planning. As a consequence, both expressive and receptive language skills should play a role in planning development.

THE REGULATIVE FUNCTION OF LANGUAGE

The act of planning implies that the actor or planner is capable of regulating her or his behavior according to the plan. The capacity to regulate one's behavior according to a plan, however, is not an inborn quality but one that develops gradually during childhood.

Levina (1979) suggests that the regulative function of children's speech appears first at the social or "interpsychological" (Vygotsky, 1978) level. In other words, children will try to regulate others' behavior with the help of speech before their self-regulative capacities emerge. Levina continues that the child's early behavior is not goal-directed in the true sense of the term; it is more likely to be influenced by factors in the external environment than by a conscious goal-directed plan. With the help of speech the child is able to "rearm" the more primitive, concrete–visual form of cognition with analytical weapons: words. As a result, the child's cognitive operations gain flexibility, freedom, and independence from the concrete stimulus field. With the help of speech, children can bring to the problem-solving process elements that are not immediately present (Díaz, Neal, & Amaya-Williams, 1990). In this way, speech allows children to liberate themselves from immanent but nonessential aspects of the environment and to focus on the essential: the representation of future action.

Before this is possible, however, a complicated developmental process occurring over most of the child's first decade of life must take place. The first stage of this process is characterized by speech that describes ongoing action, i.e., constituting speech (Levina, 1979). A positive sign of this first stage is the presence of speech that accompanies children's activity during the performance of any task. Constituting speech does not direct action but is thoroughly intertwined with other elements of a child's behavior. It does, however, play a useful role as a device for exploring and labeling the environment and accumulating experience. Gradually, and mainly through the examples of older individuals, children's speech takes on more of an indicatory role: Children begin to use speech to separate the environment into objects. This occurs first as a part of social communication and later, children do it for themselves. In this way, speech becomes an investigative tool, a mechanism for mastering the surrounding world (Levina, 1979).

It is important to note that children's behavior during the first stage may often be planful in appearance. This planfulness, however, is prelingual and more a property of the context than of the child. Speech is not used to control and regulate action but rather, to accompany it. Also, problems occurring in practical situations are solved very infrequently and only in cases (unusual at this stage) where verbal planning is observed (Levina, 1979).

At the next stage, children's speech becomes less focused on the surrounding world and more focused on their own actions. Utterances concerned with representing a problem become more noticeable and utterances having to do with verbal planning gradually begin to appear. Speech no longer merely describes action or behavior but begins to assume an inclusive character: It sums up the action in which the child is currently engaged. According to Levina (1979), this summarizing speech, which recapitulates the basic action, is the genetic precursor of planning speech. The only difference is that in planning speech, the child first formulates a plan verbally prior to carrying it out in action. In this way, the child's attempts acquire a two-phased structure: They are first prepared by a verbal plan and only then placed into action.

Planning for others is the first stage in the development of verbal planning. The first plans are positively present when a child turns to peers or adults and tells them his or her future action prior to carrying it out. At this stage it also becomes possible to stimulate verbal planning by asking children appropriate questions or giving them suggestions when they try to solve complex problems. Also, at these early stages, if children's speech is prevented, they will stop planning and their behavior will regress to an earlier level (see Sokolov, 1972, for a review of this phenomenon).

Speech that is used for planning is not simply an appendage of behavior but rather, has the essential function of guiding and directing all of the child's behavior (Levina, 1979). Like other cultural functions, verbal planning emerges first as a function created by others and directed toward others (i.e., at an interpsychological level) (Vygotsky, 1978). Then, without changing externally, it is directed toward one's own behavior in the form of egocentric speech. Finally, it is transformed by ceasing to appear externally and is abbreviated to form an internal device, namely, inner speech. For Vygotsky (1978), this latter development had significant consequences:

> The greatest change in children's capacity to use language as a problem-solving tool takes place somewhat later in their

development, when socialized speech (which has previously been used to address an adult) *is turned inward.* Instead of appealing to the adult, children appeal to themselves; language thus takes on an *intrapersonal function* in addition to its *interpersonal use.* When children develop a method of behavior for guiding themselves that had previously been used in relation to another person, when they organize their own activities according to a social form of behavior, they succeed in applying a social attitude to themselves. The history of the process of *the internalization of social speech* is also the history of the socialization of children's practical intellect (p. 27).

According to Levina (1979), children's verbal planning will assume this internal form (i.e., inner speech planning) by the age of 8 to 10. After this point, further development involves the strengthening of inner speech and the disappearance of external speech. At this later stage, external speech ceases to be a useful device in thinking and can even inhibit cognitive operations (Sokolov, 1969).

From the preceding arguments, we can conclude that the role of language or speech is essential for the development of planning in several ways. First, planning would not be possible without some form of semiotic mediation that enables both the self-regulation and the restructuring of the decision-making process—processes that are necessary for planning to occur. When signs begin to mediate the decision-making process, a new psychological process is created in which the direct impulse to react is inhibited (Lee, 1987). Instead, future action is first planned at a symbolic level prior to taking action. In this way, "the use of signs leads humans to a specific structure of behavior that breaks away from mere biological development and creates new forms of a culturally-based psychological process" (Vygotsky, 1978, p. 40).

Second, the acquisition and development of planning skills may depend on the social interactions that we enter into as well as the power of the signs that we have available for planning. If our tools for communicating are not sufficient for the task, we are unlikely to obtain the planning skills from our environment. Similarly, if our psychological tools for thinking are not powerful enough, we are unlikely to arrive at the best possible solution (Carroll, 1964). Although natural language is only one medium of communication and one source of psychological tools, it is nevertheless the most important one for both. This is especially the case after the first three years of life, which are not likely to be the most important ones for the development of planning.

DISCUSSION OF PLANNING DEVELOPMENT

Research on development of planning skills clearly indicates that there are problems associated with studying this multifaceted function in young subjects. The manner in which planning is defined and the research methods and designs used in different studies can have a decisive impact on the conclusions that are drawn. If planning is defined as deliberate means-ends behavior, then children as young as 9 months of age can be viewed as possessing rudimentary planning skills. More complex planning, requiring well-developed representational skills, can be difficult even for adolescents.

Studies using comparable definitions of planning and same-age subjects, however, have yielded remarkably similar results. Studies with infants have provided evidence of early functioning of the frontal lobes. While the tasks used in these studies hardly measure planning as it is understood in this book, the results do indicate the early emergence of intentionality and recall in guiding action. Both are necessary conditions for complex planning processes to develop later in ontogenesis. Furthermore, these studies suggest that (a) while planning requires frontal lobe functioning in order to occur, all frontal lobe functions are not related to planning and (b) Luria's (1973a) notion of the late development of the frontal lobes needs to be modified, at least to some extent, in light of these findings.

Neuropsychological studies provide little information about what occurs during the time period that Luria (1973a) identified as the beginning of frontal lobe functioning. EEG studies suggest that the frontal lobes undergo a significant growth spurt at approximately age 4, involving an expansion of anterior to posterior connections and a localized right frontal lobe growth spurt (Thatcher, 1991, 1992; Thatcher et al., 1987). Findings in the area of developmental psychology tend to support the existence of this growth spurt. According to Luria (1973a), during this same time period, children's behavior becomes increasingly verbally mediated. Based on these observations we would like to suggest that planning as a higher cognitive function emerges between the ages of 3 and 5.

But this is just the beginning, and not the end, of a long developmental process. Planning skills continue to develop both qualitatively and quantitatively. Older children can construct a functional plan more quickly, produce several alternative plans, and respond to task requirements and contextual demands more effectively than younger children. This development seems to continue well into adolescence and beyond. It also seems that this development is not linear but instead, includes several slower or faster phases. But more data is required before we can more accurately relate changes in planning to the neurophysiological changes and phases found in EEG studies.

We should remember here that planning is a higher order frontal system, as described in Chapter 3. Frontal systems receive most of their input from other parts of the brain and thus the unit of analysis is always more complex than in simple perception studies, for example. Consequently, the development of planning as a frontal system depends on the parallel or prior development of the posterior/basal systems. What occurs in the other parts of the brain and the functions supported by these areas are, according to this model, of vital importance in explaining the development of planning.

There is clearly a need for a more comprehensive theoretical model of the development of planning skills, one that would integrate the results from recent research in developmental psychology, cognitive psychology, and developmental neuropsychology. But what are the necessary components of such a model? The studies reviewed suggest several components, both intra- and interpsychological: social and contextual influences, language skills, metacognition, knowledge base, conceptual thinking, posterior/basal systems served by planning, and so forth. Searching for components for a developmental model, however, is "inherently tricky" (DeLoache & Brown, 1987). Different components may be present or absent at different ages, serve different purposes, and have different characteristics. DeLoache and Brown (1987) warn us to be cautious in concluding that the abilities and skills displayed by younger children represent early forms of the abilities and skills present in older children. Moreover, much more information is required about the development of planning as a cognitive process in general and about the relationship between planning skills and other cognitive processes (for example, attention, information coding, and language skills) during development in particular. Regardless of the form that this model might take, it would be difficult to incorporate all aspects of planning into it.

Perhaps the best course of action is to search for more limited models that concentrate on specific aspects of planning and exclude others. The PASS model of information processing introduced in Chapter 2 includes planning as a component and could therefore serve as a limited model to guide studies that concentrate on planning as a cognitive process. The model has certainly helped us to conceptualize cognitive planning and the intrapsychological factors that may influence its development. The PASS model is not, however, a comprehensive model of planning or of planning development. Before such models can be created, more data will be required on the necessary components of planning and their development.

5

Search and Planning

Search tasks provide a frame of reference for investigating planning processes and both their microgenetic and ontogenetic development. Several researchers have accepted search as a general model to investigate planning and problem solving (see, for example, Korf, 1987; Luria, 1973a; Miller et al., 1960; Newell and Simon, 1972). Miller et al. (1960), whose work was reviewed in detail in Chapter 1, suggested that we solve problems by using either a *search* or a *prediction* method. Furthermore, they proposed a distinction between *problems to prove* and *problems to find*. From our discussion about these distinctions and how they relate to planning, it was concluded that search and planning are largely interrelated concepts and that studying search will also provide us with information about planning.

Strategy deployment in search has been a major area of research. One of the first studies in the area was conducted by Sternberg (1966) using the familiar paradigm of high-speed memory search. Sternberg proposed a serial comparison process in which the input item is compared in turn to each member of the memory set. Reaction time was a function of memory set size and increased by approximately 40 milliseconds for each additional item. The dependence of reaction time on the size of the distractor items or the memory set indicates the capacity limitations of the information-processing system.

In many subsequent experiments using visual search tasks, however, it was found that search in some conditions showed either no dependence or reduced dependence on memory set size. These results held when (*a*) searching for a letter among digits or digits among letters was required (Egeth, Jonides, and Wall, 1972; Jonides and Gleitman, 1972) and (*b*) extended practice was given with a distractor set that was constant across trials (Kristofferson, 1972; Simpson, 1972; Swanson and Briggs, 1969). These findings led Shiffrin and Schneider (1977) to distinguish between two qualitatively different search processes: controlled search and automatic search or detection.

CONTROLLED AND AUTOMATIC SEARCH

Controlled processes[1] are described as being capacity-limited, flexible, and under the deliberate control of the subject, requiring both attention and effort (Estes, 1982; Shiffrin & Schneider, 1977). Automatic processes, on the other hand, are based on the activation of a learned sequence of elements in long-term memory (Schneider & Shiffrin, 1977). They are characterized as fast (Posner & Snyder, 1975), effortless (Logan, 1978; Schneider & Shiffrin, 1977), unavailable to conscious awareness (Marcel, 1983), stereotyped and resistant to change (LaBerge & Samuels, 1974), and free from attentional limitations (Hasher & Zacks, 1979; Logan, 1979, 1980). Logan (1988, pp. 492-493) summarizes automatic processing as follows:

> Automatic processing is fast and effortless because it is not subject to attentional limitations. It is automaticnomous, obligatory or uncontrollable because attentional control is exerted by allocating capacity; a process that does not require capacity cannot be controlled by allocating capacity. Finally, it is unavailable

---

[1] Readers should note that the content of this chapter for the most part reflects the view that search processes are either controlled or automatic. The hypothesis of partial automaticity is not reflected here. For studies supporting partial automaticity, see, for example, Epstein and Broota (1986) or Epstein and Lovitts (1985).

to consciousness because attention is the mechanism of consciousness and only those things that are attended are available to consciousness.

Single resource theories of attention suggest that controlled processing can become automatic with practice as a result of the gradual withdrawal of attention (Shiffrin & Schneider, 1977). With extended practice, most skills such as typing or reading are learned to the level of automaticity and performance becomes free of attentional limitations. The single resource theories of attention, however, fail to specify the learning mechanisms involved and thus "cannot make predictions about the necessity of extended practice (or anything else) in producing automaticity" (Logan & Klapp, 1991, p. 179).

Recent findings have further challenged the validity of single resource theories in explaining automatic and controlled search. Theories that emphasize the influence of multiple resources on performance limitations (Navon & Gopher, 1979; Wickens, 1984) argue that attentional resources may not be the sole determinant of controlled processing. Some researchers have gone as far as to suggest that performance may not be limited by any resources (Allport, 1980; Navon, 1984; Neisser, 1967), attentional or otherwise (Logan, 1988). Theoretically, if automatic processes occur without capacity limitations, there should be a slope of zero in the function in relation to decision speed. This is hardly found, however, and a nonzero slope represents controlled processing. Moreover, the rate of automaticity may vary relative to the complexity of task demands, which makes a qualitative distinction between controlled and automatic processing unacceptable. It is also possible that certain effects that seem to be automatic may not be so (Kahneman & Henik, 1981). For example, the Stroop effect, which is considered to be unavoidable (a condition of automaticity), becomes "much larger when the distracting information (the color name) is in the same location as the to-be-named color rather than in an adjacent location within the central fixation area" (Eysenck, 1984, p. 73).

It has also been suggested that the occurrence of automatic processing depends on the types of stimulus information to be processed. According to Treisman and Gelade (1980), automatic search processes can only be used under limited conditions. They distinguished between feature search and conjunction (object) search, and asserted that while feature search takes place automatically and in parallel, searching for objects or conjunctive targets involves serial processing as in the controlled search paradigm. They also found that lengthy practice with conjunctive features does not ensure the development of automatic processing. This "feature integration theory" has been subsequently revised in the light of search asymmetries (Treisman & Gormican, 1988). According to the modified version, feature search can be serial when close similarities exist between the target and nontargets. This suggests that it is not the stimulus attributes *per se* but the stimulus relations or similarities that may account for the presence and the degree of automatic or controlled processing in visual search.

Duncan and Humphreys (1989) go a step further and argue that similar principles control search difficulty regardless of the stimulus material. They have shown in several experiments that "search efficiency decreases with increasing similarity between targets and non-targets . . . and decreasing similarity between non-targets themselves, the two interacting to scale one another's effects" (p. 434). Their results support neither the distinction between automatic and controlled search nor the distinction between search for features and conjunctions or objects. Instead, their results imply a continuum of search efficiency involving very similar principles of search.

Perhaps the qualitative distinction between automatic and controlled search is no longer tenable. Recent evidence seems to suggest that automaticity occurs in degrees and varies along a continuum of search efficiency, requiring differing degrees of attention (Cohen, Dunbar, & McClelland, 1990) Also, it seems clear to us that the need for attentional capacity *per se* is not the sole distinguisher between automatic and controlled search, especially in the kind of visual search tasks that we have used in our experiments. Effective performance in both search forms demands at least some level of arousal or attentiveness, as well as sufficient coding skills to distinguish the target stimulus from nontargets. In addition, controlled search seems to demand a search strategy, that is, a plan of how to scan the search field and distinguish effectively between the target and nontargets belonging to the same stimulus category. If this is true, then controlled search would be a planning task, whereas automatic search would be an attention (arousal) task. Consequently, the differences between the two could be regarded as experimental examples of the shift from one cognitive process (planning) to the other (attention)

EXPERIMENTS ON VISUAL SEARCH

There are two basic research questions implied above. The first pertains to the demonstration of a shift from automatic to controlled search, in other words, that there are differences between the two (although more minor than the automatic-controlled paradigm suggests). Also, since both automatic and controlled search exert cognitive processing demands, we should be able to manipulate them (although not to the same degree) by changing the perceptual organization and structural demands of the search field (for example, mapping condition, density, target location, and stimulus features) that determine the extent of search difficulty.

The second research question pertains to identifying and postulating mechanisms and processes involved in search as well as their ontogenetic and microgenetic development as they affect the rate of search. For example, if controlled search demands planning and automatic search depends only on arousal, different developmental patterns should be visible across age. Moreover, priming or providing cues through instruction should facilitate controlled search to a greater extent than automatic search. In the experiments that follow, we have made an attempt to study search processes by examining the role of these variables.

THE VISUAL SEARCH TASK

Our main tool for studying search processes has been the Visual Search task that was originally introduced by Teuber, Battersby, and Bender (1949, 1951) to identify search deficits after cerebral lesion. This test has been found to be especially sensitive to frontal lobe lesions (Teuber, 1964) and is therefore consistent with the paradigm of planning as a frontal system that was advocated in Chapter 3.

Figure 5.1 shows two examples of a typical Visual Search task used in our studies. Two mapping conditions are presented, automatic (left) and controlled (right). In the automatic search condition, the target and the distractors belong to different stimulus categories (for example, a letter among numbers or a word among pictures), whereas in the controlled search condition, the target and the distractors

Figure 5.1
Visual Search Items

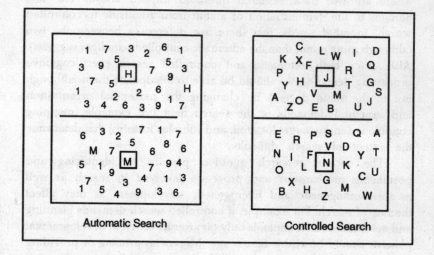

belong to the same stimulus category (for example, a letter among letters), thus increasing the attentional and coding demands of the task. Both of these conditions can also vary in field density, that is, in the number of distractors in the response field. Both tasks in Figure 5.1 are low-density tasks and contain approximately 25 distractors from which the subject must identify the target. High-density search fields contain two times as many distractors as low-density search fields, which, of course, decreases search efficiency. At the center of each response field is a circled target that appears only once in the field of distracting items surrounding the target. The subject's task is to find an instance of the target as quickly as possible and her or his score is the time taken to find the target.

Visual Search was originally identified as an appropriate measure of planning by Ashman (1978) and Ashman and Das (1980). Controlled search has since been used as a measure of planning in several studies and has consistently loaded on the planning factor (see, for example, Naglieri & Das, 1988; Naglieri, Das, Stevens, & Ledbetter, 1991; Naglieri, Prewett, & Bardos, 1989).

EFFECTS OF STRUCTURAL FACTORS, STIMULUS CATEGORY, AND AGE

The first visual search experiment (Kar, 1989; Kar and Dash, 1988) investigated the effects of mapping condition (automatic and controlled), field density (high and low), and field stimuli (pictures, numbers, or letters) on the efficiency of search. The effects of mapping condition and field density are well established in the research literature (Schneider & Shiffrin, 1977; Shiffrin & Schneider, 1977; Treisman & Gelade, 1980). Our purpose was to determine if these effects, derived from high-speed computer search and scanning, would also manifest in the simpler paper and pencil task shown in Figure 5.1. The second objective was to determine if there was a relationship between the rate of search, naming time, and the naming strategy used by the subject in encoding the items in the search field. A third objective concerned developmental changes. Subjects from different age groups were used to determine whether relationships between experimental variables would change with subjects' developmental level.

The sample consisted of 90 subjects, 30 from each of grades 5, 7 and 9, who were 10 to 11, 12 to 13, and 13 to 14 years of age, respectively. A basic version of the Visual Search task was used and consisted of sixteen 22 cm X 28 cm cards, each of which had a line across its center that divided the card into two response fields. In automatic search, the target was a number among pictures or a picture among numbers. In controlled search, the target was a picture among pictures or a letter among letters. Both of these mapping conditions also varied in field density: half of the cards in each condition had a high density of distractors and the other half had a low density of distractors.

Naming strategy was evaluated using a 5-point Naming Attempt rating scale that assessed subjects' inclination to name the stimuli during the course of search. After the completion of the Visual Search task, each subject was asked if he or she was naming the stimuli while searching. A rating of ·1 indicated that the subject was always naming the stimuli, 2, most of the time, 3, sometimes, 4, rarely, and 5, that the subject was not naming at all.

Subjects' naming time was assessed using Picture Naming and Letter Naming tasks. For the Picture Naming task, 30 pictures were randomly selected from among those in the Visual Search controlled condition. They were reproduced so that five pictures appeared in each of the six rows on a page. Pictures were randomly distributed on three separate pages. The subject's task was to name the pictures as quickly as possible. The average time taken to name all of the pictures on the three pages was used as the picture-naming time. The Letter Naming task was prepared following the same procedure used for the Picture Naming task.

Visual Search scores were first subjected to a 3 (Grade) X 2 (Mapping Conditions) X 2 (Field Density) analysis of variance. The main findings of this analysis can be summarized as follows:

1. Automatic search was significantly faster than controlled search. As expected, subjects took significantly less time to locate the target when the target and nontargets belonged to different stimulus categories than when both came from the same stimulus category.

2. The main effect of Grade was significant. Developmental differences seemed to be more prominent in controlled than in automatic search but the Grade X Mapping Condition interaction was not significant.

3. Interaction of Mapping Condition and Field Density was significant. Field Density had a significant effect on controlled search (searching the target was faster in a low-density than in a high-density field) but the same was not true for automatic search.

4. Grade showed a significant interaction with Field Density: Grade differences were more prominent in the high than in the low density condition.

Subsequently, two 3 (Grade) X 2 (Field Stimuli) X 2 (Field Density) ANOVAs were performed, one each for automatic and controlled search. The main findings of these analyses were:

5. The main effect of Field Stimuli was significant in both automatic and controlled search, showing different effects for pictures and numbers as background stimuli. Post hoc tests (Scheffé test) revealed that Field Stimuli had a significant effect in the high-density condition but not in low-density condition. In automatic search, pictures were easier to find among numbers than were numbers among pictures. In controlled search, search for pictures among pictures was slower than search for letters among letters.

The effects of Picture and Letter Naming time, and naming strategy were computed separately for automatic and controlled search. All of these analyses yielded the same results.

6. Individual differences in naming time and naming strategy did not affect search efficiency.

These results indicate that the characteristics of search found in high-speed computer scanning can be generalized to a paper and pencil Visual Search test. We can probably import the explanation given in the computer tasks as well. For example, we found that the occurrence of automaticity seems to depend on complex operations relating to target and nontarget relationship, as Duncan and Humphreys (1989) have shown. Furthermore, a number target among pictures took longer to find than a picture target among numbers. According to Duncan and Humphreys (see foregoing), search efficiency decreases as dissimilarity between nontargets increases. Our results suggest that, for our subjects, pictures were more dissimilar than numbers as nontargets. Numbers are much more familiar to subjects than pictures. This familiarity arises as a result of experiencing repeated instances of numbers but not the "strange little pictures". The "traces" of numbers are readily available in memory and are stocked with many instances. How these traces were formed in memory is perhaps unimportant.

Another, not necessarily contradictory, explanation is that the encoding demands of the distracting field affect search efficiency, even when the target and the distractors belong to different categories. Considering a picture in a field of numbers, the encoding demands of the distractor stimuli (i.e., nontarget numbers) trigger off automatic attentional responses. Consequently, the rate of nontarget rejection is more rapid and the search is more efficient than when the distractor is more laborious to encode (for example, a picture). This finding is supported by the results of the controlled search, where searching for a picture among pictures was slower than searching for a letter among letters. Could this be due to the fact that the encoding of pictures takes longer than the encoding of letters, which in turn takes longer than the encoding of numbers (Denckla & Rudel, 1976; Eaking & Douglas, 1971)? Although this might be a plausible explanation, an anomaly was evident in that neither naming competence (time) nor naming attempt (strategy) influenced search in our experiment. This result suggests that although the influence of naming demands cannot be ruled out, naming may not have been the prevalent encoding mechanism for our subjects. Later in this chapter we will introduce another study that dealt more directly with the naming problem.

The fact that automatic search was affected by background stimuli but not by field density poses an interesting question: if encoding demands of the stimuli affect the rate of search, should not an increase in the number of stimuli to be encoded also lead to an increase in search time? Yes, it should, but only if we assume that the subject encodes every nontarget stimulus in the search field (or all stimuli preceding the finding of the target figure). Perhaps this is not the case, however, and the subject encodes only a few nontarget stimuli before forming a representation of the category that they belong to and how that category is different from the target stimulus. After this initial representation, the search would proceed without detailed encoding and consequently, increasing the number of nontarget stimuli would not decrease search efficiency. In controlled search, however, this "automaticity of encoding" is not possible since target and nontarget stimuli belong to the same category. Accordingly, an increase in the number of non-target stimuli will lead to a decrease in search efficiency, as we noticed.

An important finding of the present experiment is the development of search efficiency with increasing age and grade. Grade differences were significant both in automatic and controlled search, indicating that the development of automaticity is a gradual rather than an all-or-none event. These developmental differences were also found in two other experiments reported below. These results will also be discussed at the end of this chapter.

We believe that the automaticity question is an important one for many school-related skills such as reading and arithmetic. These skills, when overlearned, can be retrieved automatically from memory. This releases attentional resources to other aspects of tasks, such as understanding the gist of a story or planning and regulating the total solution for a mathematical problem. Perhaps for basic addition and multiplication, automatic, extended practice involving doing and rote learning not only have the same results but involve overlapping actions. While doing, children engage in frequent overt rehearsals, which is the essence of rote learning. For instance, can learning make the visual search for a number among other numbers become automatic if the number target occurs at the same location in the search field trial after trial? This was one of the questions considered in the next experiment.

TARGET–LOCATION RELATIONSHIP

Treisman and Gormican (1988) suggested that feature search precedes localization. Search for the location may, however, be unnecessary in automatic search because of the "pop-out" effect. In contrast, in controlled search, which usually proceeds serially, searching for the location of the target is imperative. This implies that searching for location imposes constraints on search efficiency and that part of the individual variability in search efficiency can be explained by differences in search strategies. In our Visual Search task, such constraints can be verified and manipulated by varying the relationship between the target and its location across trials. In Experiment 2 (Nanda, 1990), we wanted to show that when the target and its location remain the same across trials, automatic attentional responses manifest even in controlled search. That is, a continuum of search efficiency can be established by varying the consistency of the target-location relationship across trials, thereby minimizing the role of search strategies in determining search efficiency.

A variation of the search task involving 24 cards was designed for this purpose. Three mapping conditions were used: simple automatic search (a number target among dots), automatic search (a number target among pictures) and controlled search (a number target among numbers). For each mapping condition there were two levels of density: high and low. For each density level, the relationship between the target and its location was manipulated in four different ways: (a) target different and location different, (b) target same and location different, (c) target different and location same, and (d) target same and location same.

In all, 120 grade 8 students (12 to 13 years of age) were administered the task. The four conditions representing variations in the target-location relationship were administered to each subject in a predetermined random order. The conditions were equally distributed among subjects in their order of presentation. In each condition, however, the simple automatic cards were given first, followed by automatic cards and controlled cards, with low-density cards preceding high-density cards.

A repeated measures ANOVA, with visual search time as the dependent variable and Search Condition (3), Field Density (2), and Target-Location Relationship (4) as independent variables, was employed.

The results showed that the main effects of Search Condition, Field Density, and Target-Location Relationship were all significant. Furthermore, a significant interaction between Search Condition and Field Density indicated that simple automatic search, automatic search, and controlled search were affected differently by the two field density conditions. Mean search times indicated that the effect was most pronounced in controlled search, whereas in simple automatic search there was no effect.

Post hoc comparisons (Scheffé test) indicated the existence of a continuum of search efficiency. Simple automatic search was significantly faster than automatic search, which in turn was faster than controlled search. It was also found that search was significantly faster when the target location was the same across trials than when the target location was changed. This was true for all three mapping conditions, although the interaction between Search Condition and Target-Location Relationship was significant. Comparison of means indicated that the differences were most prominent in the controlled search condition.

When the subject perceives the consistency of the target location, search efficiency is accelerated due to the limited search space. This effect was most prominent in the controlled search condition, which (according to our rationale) demands a more strategic approach than, for example, automatic search. Controlled search is no longer serial when the location of the target is kept constant and thus the strategy of search is given *a priori* to subjects. The results also point out that even automatic responses were affected by inconsistency of location across trials. The degree of interference of the nontargets was reduced when the subject knew where to attend: "Filtering costs are caused by the processing of events rather than by the mere pressure of irrelevant items. They are eliminated by advance information about the location of the target" (Kahneman, Treisman, and Burkell, 1983, p. 510). In the next experiment we tried to manipulate the location of the target in different zones (i.e., the border or center) of the search field.

EDGE EFFECTS AND PRIOR KNOWLEDGE

Studies of "edge effects" in visual search reveal that search is faster when the target is located in the central zone than when it is located in the border region of the search field. It has also been suggested that in a search field with minimal discriminability between the target and the nontargets, attention is focused serially on one clump of items after another (Treisman and Gormican, 1988) and "the more discriminable the targets and non-targets, the larger can be the clumps" (Duncan and Humphreys, 1989, p. 434). In our Visual Search task, the target sample always appears in the center of the search field. This implies that the subject's initial attention is focused on the center of the search field and that search may proceed from a smaller clump in the center outward toward the border. Thus, search may be faster when the target is located in the central zone than when it appears on the border of the search field. Furthermore, different quadrangles of the search field may be attended to in different order, especially if the search is guided by a plan of action. If the search follows the same eye-movement model as occurs in reading English, for example, then it would proceed from left to right and from top to bottom. Another viable option is to first search one side of the search field, probably from top to bottom, and to then search the other side.

In the third experiment (Mohapatra, 1990), we controlled both the zone and the quadrangle of the target in order to determine whether the search pattern favors one zone and/or one quadrangle over the other. The second objective of this experiment was to test the effect of prior knowledge of the target location, that is, the effect of priming on search efficiency. Several studies have found that advance knowledge of the location of the target increases search efficiency by eliminating or reducing the interfering effects of irrelevant stimuli (Kahneman et al., 1983; Posner, 1978; Treisman, 1982). Priming should also reduce demand for an efficient search strategy since the search is limited by prior knowledge of the target location. We wanted to test this by creating a priming condition in which subjects were given a clue about the location of the target prior to search. A third objective of the experiment was to explore the sensitivity of these effects to development. On the basis of earlier findings

(Kar, 1989; Kar and Dash, 1988), it was predicted that search speed would increase with age.

Ninety subjects, 30 from each of grades five (9 to 10 years of age), seven (11 to 12 years of age), and nine (13 to 14 years of age), were given a modified version of the controlled Visual Search task. In this experiment, we used sixteen 22 cm X 28 cm cards equally divided into two levels of density. The target was a "Q" inserted in a square in the center of the search field, which contained letters from A to Z that were randomly and proportionately distributed on the surface of the card. On half of the cards for each density level, the target was located on the border, whereas for the other half, the target was located near the center of the search field. The border/center location appeared equally in each of the four quadrangles of the field.

The test was administered to each subject under two conditions of instruction: standard and priming. In the standard condition, subjects were instructed to find the target as quickly as possible. In the priming condition, the experimenter added a clue about which side of the search field (left or right) might contain the target. Half of the subjects in each group received the standard instruction first, followed by the priming condition and the other half were tested in the reverse order.

Analysis of variance, with search time as the dependent variable and Grade (3), Priming (2), and Field Density (2) as independent variables, was calculated first. As expected, the results showed search to be faster with development, for the low-density field, and with priming. Also, the interaction effects of Grade and Priming, Grade and Field Density, and Priming and Density were all significant. The effect of priming was more pronounced in the high-density condition and for the youngest subjects.

Analysis of variance with search time as the dependent variable and Grade (3), Zone (2), and Location of target (4 quadrangles) as independent variables showed that Grade and Zone had significant main effects, whereas Location did not.

Separate ANOVAs for low- and high-density search, with search time as the dependent variable and Grade, Priming, and Location as independent variables, showed that whereas Grade and Priming had significant main effects in both conditions, the main effect of location was significant for low-density search but not for high-density search.

These results support the conclusions of earlier studies that the search process is malleable. The cost of filtering in visual search can be reduced by manipulating the structural features of the search field. The critical aspect of the findings, however, relates to the effect of priming. When a subject is provided with a cue about the location of the target, search is faster. Prior knowledge prompts subjects to develop a plan of action that substantially increases their efforts to attend to relevant stimuli and thereby decreases the interfering effects of the distracting field. A good plan increases the subject's conscious control of the strategic demands involved and reduces the "cost of filtering" in search. In the high-density condition and especially for younger subjects, who are more susceptible to the interfering effects of the distracting stimuli, the beneficial effects of such a plan of action are relatively higher. We believe that this finding has implications for mediated learning experiences that affect search efficiency and for the development of programs to help younger children to develop better planning skills.

The location of the target within different quadrangles of the search field had an effect only when the search field contained a low density of distractors. Perhaps somewhat surprisingly, quadrangle 2 (i.e., top right corner) was usually associated with the slowest responses, indicating that subjects' searches did not generally proceed from left to right as reading does. Our results did not, however, indicate that any other order would have been predominant among subjects. This may have been due to significant individual variability in search plans: Perhaps different subjects have different preferences for dividing the search field and proceeding.

WORD SEARCH

The above experiments clearly show developmental changes in search efficiency when relatively simple stimuli (for example, numbers, letters) are used. In the fourth experiment (Pattnaik, 1992), an attempt was made to determine if the principles of search manifested in the detection of simple stimuli could be generalized to more complex stimuli (words) and to see if this type of search was also sensitive to developmental changes. Both of these effects were expected on the basis of previous research (see, for example, Fisk & Schneider, 1983).

A Word Search task was designed according to the pattern of the Visual Search task used in Experiment 1. Two- and three-letter Oriya words, representing two levels of complexity, were selected from textbooks used by students in grades one, two, and three. The task consisted of 16 cards: 8 cards that contained two-letter words and 8 cards that contained three-letter words. In both cases, both simple (4 cards) and complex (4 cards) words were used. Each of the resulting four categories included two automatic search cards and two controlled search cards, with a high-density card and a low-density card included in both conditions. For the automatic search condition, the distracting stimuli were pictures. All 16 cards were administered individually to 150 subjects, with 50 subjects from each of grades 5 (8 to 9 years of age), 7 (10 to 11 years of age), and 9 (12 to 13 years of age).

Four different ANOVAs, with Grade (3), Word Complexity (2), and Field Density (2) as independent variables, were calculated, with one for each of the following four conditions: automatic search time for two-letter words, controlled search time for two-letter words, automatic search time for three-letter words, and controlled search time for three-letter words.

The main effect of Grade was significant in all four conditions. Older children generally performed better than younger children for both simple and complex words, and for both mapping conditions. Grade effects, however, seemed to be more prominent in controlled than in automatic search.

Word complexity had a significant main effect for all of the conditions except automatic search time for three-letter words. Field density also had a significant main effect in all four analyses: High density search required a longer period of time in all four conditions. This result contradicts the finding of Experiment 1 above, in which automatic search showed no effect of field density. The results also showed that automatic search was faster than controlled search under all conditions, supporting earlier findings for simple stimuli.

These results indicate that search principles derived from the detection of simple stimuli can be generalized to the more complex processing involved in word search. This finding may have implications for understanding reading; however, several questions remain unanswered. How does the word search become automatic? What are the processes underlying word search? Which of these processes are sensitive to developmental changes and intervention? These are some of the questions that will need to be examined in future research.

Naming, Search, and Planning

Planning is "blind" without adequately coded information. Moreover, different planning tasks may demand different coding processes and knowledge about specific coding skills can be a prerequisite for their successful completion. For example, while searching, the subject must identify the relevant object in the search space and distinguish it from irrelevant objects. Perhaps the most common means of identifying relevant objects is to name them, in other words, to attach to them a verbal label that distinguishes their specific features or that places them in a certain category (Luria, 1966).

Consequently, the rate of search may be influenced by the speed at which the stimuli are named. The relationship between naming and search, however, may be affected by (a) the nature of the task, (b) the subject's search and naming strategy, and (c) the subject's inclination to name in the first place. If a task demands strategies other than naming and the subject is inclined to name the stimulus, this would be detrimental to his or her performance. For example, Kearins (1981, 1986) showed that Australian aboriginal children consistently outperformed European Australian children in complex visuo-spatial memory tasks. Aboriginal children showed very little evidence of naming and instead, seemed to rely on visual memory strategies. In contrast, European Australian children tried to employ memory strategies grounded in verbal mediation, which were not effective in Kearins' tasks.

On the other hand, when naming is intrinsic to the task demands, faster naming should accelerate the rate of search. In Experiment 1, however, neither naming time nor naming attempt were found to influence visual search performance. This indicates that naming may not be necessary for successful completion of the Visual Search task. In the following experiment, we examined the relationship between naming and performance in a different search task in which naming is obligatory.

Matching Numbers was developed by Naglieri and Das (1987) to measure planning by virtue of the need for an efficient system of determining which of two numbers match. It has loaded consistently on the planning factor in recent research (Naglieri & Das, 1988; Naglieri et al., 1991). Figure 5.2 shows a typical example of a Matching Numbers task. The version used in this study was divided into three parts. Each part contained 48 numbers, with six numbers appearing in each of eight rows. Part I consisted of two- and three-digit numbers, Part II consisted of four-, five-, and six-digit numbers, and Part III consisted of six- and seven-digit numbers. The subject's task was to find and circle the two numbers that were the same in each of the eight rows appearing on a page. In order to do this efficiently, subjects had to code (usually by naming all or part of each number) while trying to match two numbers and disregard distractors. Thus, individual and developmental differences in matching time should be influenced by number naming competence. The lower the number naming time, the lower the matching time should be.

Figure 5.2
An Example of Matching Numbers

19	23	26	18	23
34	51	17	34	37
365	356	366	635	365
549	459	495	459	594
1793	7193	7139	7193	1739
8247	8724	8427	8274	8427

In order to test these hypotheses, the Matching Numbers task and the Number Naming task were presented to 90 male subjects, 30 each from grades 5, 7, and 9, from an urban public school in Bhubaneswar, Orissa. The Number Naming task was devised to measure simple number naming time. Ninety numbers, 30 from each of the three parts of the Matching Numbers task, were randomly selected and reproduced on a page with five numbers in each of the six rows. The subject's task was to name the numbers as quickly as possible. The time taken to name each page was recorded separately and was used as the number naming time for that digit-density level.

After each subject had completed the Matching Numbers task, he was also asked what strategy one should follow while matching the numbers. A three-point rating scale was devised to assess each subject's matching strategy by evaluating his report. A rating of 1 indicated that the subject was comparing each number as a whole with the other numbers. A rating of 2 indicated that he was naming the first and the last digits of numbers while matching; a rating of 3 indicated responses other than 1 or 2.

The main results of this study can be summarized as follows:

1. Number naming time decreased with increasing grade.
2. Subjects who were faster in naming numbers were also faster in matching numbers, particularly in the high digit-density condition.
3. Matching time for subjects using a specific strategy (comparing the first and the last digits of the numbers) was found to be shorter than for subjects using other strategies.

The study clearly indicates that automaticity in naming and identifying numbers facilitates number matching performance in the Matching Numbers task, whereas the same was not true for the Visual Search task. It appears that subjects used strategies other than naming in Visual Search. Both Matching Numbers and Visual Search are marker tests of planning and both involve searching for a target. At least some of the strategic demands underlying them, however, are different, indicating that search is not a unified construct. Thus, when investigating the development of search, it is not age or grade as such but the concomitant growth of cognitive processes and their relative contribution to the development of search efficiency that should be the focus of future research (Kar & Dash, 1992).

An important finding in this study is the relationship between specific strategy and efficiency in number-matching performance. Subjects using a specific matching strategy performed relatively better in Matching Numbers than subjects who used other naming strategies. This reflects the importance of individual differences in strategy utilization as a major source of variability in search as a cognitive process (Belmont and Mitchell, 1987; Brown and Deloache, 1978). A major portion of the developmental changes in cognitive functions can be attributed to changes in strategies, plans, and programs, and their use by children. The relationship between qualitative changes in task-specific strategy use and cognitive growth, however, requires further research.

THE EFFECTS OF SCHOOLING AND VERBALIZATION

Boundary conditions and developmental changes in search reported in the studies listed in the foregoing discussion may be confounded with schooling. The relationship between planning and school learning has been found to be weaker than the relationship between coding (simultaneous and successive processing) and school achievement (Das, 1988; Das and Dash, 1990). Also, in factor analytic studies, planning does not necessarily emerge as a separate factor for unschooled children as early as it does for schooled children (Das and Dash, 1990). These observations prompted us to consider whether there is a performance difference between schooled and unschooled children in searching, and if such a difference exists, how it relates to their coding skills.

To address these questions, a study was designed to examine the cognitive competence of schooled and unschooled children on measures of simultaneous and successive processing, and planning (Kar and Nanda, 1993). Das (1988) suggests that most school learning relates to coding but not to planning skills. This led us to expect that although there may be significant performance differences between schooled and unschooled children on information coding tasks, performance differences in searching, especially when a simple perceptual task is used, should be minimal.

The assessment of unschooled children using standardized testing procedures is problematic. Differences in performance, often favoring schooled children, may be partly attributable to their familiarity with such procedures. In order to control for any performance differences that might arise from the use of standardized assessment procedures, we chose to use both standardized and Dynamic Assessment (DA) procedures. Dynamic Assessment procedures have been found to be beneficial in optimizing cognitive performance (Brown and Campione, 1986; Carlson and Wiedl, 1988; Feuerstein, 1979). Our design also allowed us to assess the effect of minimal prompting, which is included in the DA procedure, on subjects' performance.

The sample consisted of 40 children who were 12 to 14 years of age. Half of the subjects were seventh graders in a rural school in Orissa and the other half were unschooled children from the same area who shared an equivalent sociocultural environment. The tasks included a brief version of the Visual Search task (i.e., four automatic and four controlled search cards); Tokens, which is a measure of verbal simultaneous processing; and Successive Ordering, which is a measure of nonverbal successive processing (Naglieri .& Das, 1988).

Both the schooled and the unschooled subjects (N=20 in each group) were randomly assigned to two groups. All subjects were first tested according to the standard procedure for each task. After a five-minute rest period during which subjects engaged in conversation with the experimenter, 10 schooled children and 10 unschooled children were tested again following the standard procedure. The other 10 subjects from each group were given the following instructions in their native language (i.e., Oriya): "You are already familiar with the task. I am asking you to do it again just as before, but before we start again, I would like you to tell me how you are going to proceed with the task and why you would do what you would at each step of the task. Now please tell me about it." After these instructions subjects verbalized for five minutes and the experimenter probed them about their reasons for the strategies that they wanted to employ. No other intervention or prompts were used. After verbalization, subjects were administered each of the three tests following the standard procedure.

The results can be summarized as follows:

1. Schooled children were significantly better in simultaneous and successive processing than unschooled children.
2. Schooled children performed better than unschooled children in automatic search, whereas there was no difference between the two groups in controlled search.
3. The DA procedure did not have a facilitating effect on planning and successive processing scores, whereas it significantly affected performance on the Tokens task, which is a verbal simultaneous processing task.

The above results support the view that processes facilitated by school learning (i.e., simultaneous and successive modes of information processing) differentiate between schooled and unschooled children better than planning processes, which are not as much a part of normal school learning. The positive effect of schooling on verbal simultaneous processing was expected as verbal material constitutes the dominant content in school learning. Also, school subjects like geometry, mathematics, and language arts emphasize the perception of logical relationships, which facilitates simultaneous processing. The Successive Ordering task, in which order memory (i.e., recalling the order of locations) is critical, also differentiated between schooled and unschooled children. This result supports earlier findings by Rogoff (1981), who suggests that school is probably one of the few environments in which an individual has to deliberately remember information as a goal in itself.

Schooled and unschooled children also differed in automatic search but not in controlled search. This surprising result may be explained by the fact that in the automatic search condition, the distractors were numbers, which are much more familiar to schooled than to unschooled children. On the other hand, the distracting field stimuli in the controlled search condition were pictures that are probably equally familiar to both groups, thus making the cost of filtering approximately equal.

Although our results support the earlier suggestion that school learning enhances coding skills more than planning skills (Das, 1988), the limited nature of our study does not justify a conclusion that school learning does not contribute to the development of planning skills over and above that which occurs as a result of maturation and development alone. More studies with a wider variety of planning tasks would be needed before firmer conclusions could be drawn.

The results also provided evidence that strategy verbalization facilitated performance when the experimental task demanded a verbal mode of processing simultaneous relationships but the same was not true for the Visual Search task. In the Visual Search task, the number of alternative strategies is large and subjects may constrict their search by using various criteria for strategy selection (Shiffrin & Schneider, 1977; Treisman, 1982). As a result, verbalization, as a strategy, may have a minimal impact on search efficiency. Kar, Dash, Das and Carlson (1993) examined the effects of verbalization with a different planning task, Number Finding (Naglieri and Das, 1988), which is more structured and possesses a larger number of constraints (presumably involving different planning strategies) than Visual Search. Interestingly, Kar et al. found that verbalization had a facilitative effect on planning processes in the Number Finding task. They suggested that the increased efficiency in the Number Finding task resulted from greater coding efficiency and better deployment of selective attention and search strategies as a result of verbalization. Luria (1973a) suggested that verbalization helps conscious regulation of behavior when a strategy is explicit. High task constraints probably make Number Finding easier to regulate consciously than Visual Search. In Visual Search, the strategy may not be explicit even after verbalization or the verbalized strategy is not necessarily the one guiding the subject's performance. In both cases, a DA procedure would not lead to enhanced performance.

It is also possible that planning may become relatively automatic with practice, a suggestion that has been made by several researchers (see, for example, Das, 1989; De Lisi, 1987). Accordingly, some forms of planning may not always be accessible to introspection. In simple tasks such as Visual Search, the strategy (for example, scanning the page in some systematic way) may already have become completely automatic due to extensive practice with different types of real-life search tasks. When planning has become automatic, subjects can have great difficulty in verbally reporting how they solved the task even though their performance may clearly be planful. But the same problem may also result from a task involving too many variables. Broadbent, Fitzgerald, and Broadbent (1986) reported that their subjects were not able to describe the strategies that they used in solving complex and novel tasks requiring judgement and decision making. The authors suggested that tasks in which the crucial aspects are many and latent in a mass of less relevant data are best tackled by using "implicit experience". That is, such tasks are best dealt with by matching the current situation with a similar one from the past and selecting action based on previous experience. When the problem is solved by using this "look-up table" method, the discrepancy between the subject's verbal knowledge and her or his planning performance is often significant. The other way to consider this is to postulate that when the planning situation involves a search between relatively unlimited numbers of alternatives, we will have to limit the search by using some type of heuristic. The most common heuristic involves relying on previous experience and "intuition".

DISCUSSION OF SEARCH AND PLANNING

In the studies reported above we have tried to establish that simple search tasks, such as Visual Search, are valuable instruments for studying the variables affecting planning. Our results indicate that the same characteristics of search can be found in paper and pencil Visual Search tasks that have been reported in high-speed computer scanning tasks.

By using different types of tasks, some of. which are quite different from those that are generally found in the visual search literature, we have shown how structural properties of the search space influence the deployment of strategies and how search efficiency can be manipulated both by changing perceptual organizational factors and by inducing a plan of action through instruction. Thus, planning components of search are clearly malleable and a continuum of search efficiency (Duncan and Humphreys, 1989) can be generated by changing the structural properties of the task.

Futhermore, search and planning are clearly sensitive to development, as several of our studies demonstrate. Search becomes faster with development. This effect is especially prominent in controlled search but is also present in automatic search. What develops, however, is still largely an unanswered question.

We believe that some of these developmental changes may relate to the development of simultaneous and successive coding skills: with increasing age, the degree of automaticity in stimulus encoding increases. It has been suggested that coding processes are a prerequisite for planning (Das, 1980). While searching, the subject must discriminate the target from nontargets as well as recognize it. Thus, coding processes are essential for searching. Whether the development of these skills is associated predominantly with learning experiences, neural development, or the interaction of these two processes, is a pertinent question. Can we say, for example, that partial encoding of nontargets, resulting in faster rejection, develops with extended practice? This could be tested by using the three mapping conditions mentioned in Experiment 2 (i.e., simple automatic search, automatic search, and controlled search) for different grade levels and then comparing the developmental trends in different mapping conditions. One can hardly expect that practice with dots (in simple automatic search) would lead to faster rejection of nontargets. But do we learn to reject picture targets as quickly as numbers in controlled search because of extensive practice?

Successful search may depend on attentional resources and their control because some amount of attentional resources must be available to subjects and must be voluntarily mobilized by them in order to find the target. With increasing age and educational experience, children seem to develop better control of their attentional resources and learn to select more successful strategies for dealing with distracting stimuli in the search field. We observed that age-related changes in search strategies probably accounted for much of the improvement in performance shown by our subjects. To arrive at firm conclusions, however, we need to collect protocol data from different age groups during the search task. Protocol data would better reveal the strategies that children use, especially while engaged in more difficult controlled search.

In sum, our studies showed that planful behavior evolves not only with changing search strategies but also with the development of encoding and attentional processes. This implies that the development of coding and attentional processes is intimately related to the development of planning functions. According to Luria (1973a), all cognitive activity involves the concerted participation of the three functional units of the brain: the first of which is responsible for attention, the second for coding, and the third for planning. Thus, the development of planning and search cannot be studied in isolation but only in relation to the concomitant growth of attentional and coding processes (Das, Naglieri, & Kirby, 1994).

The various paradigms for visual search that we have discussed can be used in studying derangements in planful behavior observed among neuropsychological patients. Visual Search tasks have been used for some time as diagnostic tools in identifying patients with brain lesions. This line of clinical research owes a great deal to Teuber (see, for example, Teuber, 1964; Teuber, Battersby, and Bender, 1949, 1951). He found that the speed of visual search was slower, particularly for patients with a frontal lobe lesion, as compared to patients with more posterior lesions. Teuber also found that visual search can be used as a test of hemisphericity. Several researchers have continued this line of research (see, for example, Eglin, Robertson, and Knight, 1991; Grabowecky, Robertson, and Treisman, 1993 for more recent examples). We suggest that the series of experiments that we have presented can provide material for testing subtle deficits other than slow response speed that result from frontal lobe injury. One might ask, for example, if it can be assumed, as in the normal population, that no qualitative difference would be found between automatic and controlled search and that instead, there would be a continuum of search efficiency guided by common principles. Similarly, using different stimuli such as pictures, numbers, letters, or even words, might inform us about the location of the lesion. Do certain locations, for example, compel frontal lobe patients to use an uneconomical strategy in searching for a picture among pictures, such that they have to encode the name of the picture before they can compare it with the target and accept or reject it? Or do lesions in more posterior areas affect word search differently than number search? Thus, we recommend the use of these simple paper and pencil tasks as tools for investigating differences and impairments in planning.

6

CONCEPTUAL PLANNING

There is an informal test in Luria's classic work on the disturbance of planning functions due to frontal lobe injury: A picture depicting a scene from a ski resort is shown to a person. The picture contains the usual skiers, flags, people eating ice-cream, and a pool of water with the sign, "Danger, thin ice". A man has just fallen into this pool of water and several people are trying to help him. When asked to describe what is happening in the picture, the individual with frontal lobe dysfunction cannot focus on the central theme of the picture, the critical element. Instead, he or she describes the setting, that is, the scenery.

In the context of the PASS theory, planning, like the two information coding processes and attention, can be measured by tests that are predominantly perceptual, mnestic (memory), or conceptual. The telling of the story associated with the picture is done at the conceptual level. In contrast, Visual Search, which was described in great detail in the previous chapter, involves the perceptual level and Matching Numbers is likely a combination of both perceptual and memory abilities.

In this chapter, we will discuss a series of studies that have mainly used two planning tasks at the conceptual level. These tasks are Crack-the-Code and Planned Composition. Both of these tasks differ considerably in their form and content from tasks presented in the previous chapter but they also differ considerably from each other. They have, however, been consistently shown to correlate with the more simple planning tasks such as Visual Search. Let us begin by introducing the tasks.

PLANNED COMPOSITION

In planned composition typically a picture such as the one described earlier is shown, and the individual is asked to write or describe what is happening in the picture. In our previous research a different picture was used: it was a picture of a man ploughing a field, a pair of horses, and a woman looking at the scene. She appears to be holding some books and is visibly pregnant. The subject is asked to write a story on one page or to tell it into a tape recorder. The instruction for the subject is to tell us what is happening, what led it to happen, and what will happen in the future. But, essentially, the person is free to write or tell a story, the picture merely being a stimulus. The picture is usually vague and there is no right or wrong story to be written. Then the composition is evaluated not only on the basis of grammar but also in terms of organization and uniqueness. Table 6.1 presents the evaluation system for the composition.

In our research (Das, 1980, 1984a), Planned Composition was found to be correlated with perceptual planning tasks such as Visual Search and Trail Making, which is a combination of perceptual and memory abilities. The correlation was not a very strong one, however, because composition is, after all, much more heterogeneous in terms of the processes that it uses than simpler tasks such as Visual Search or Trail Making. The point, however, is that a good part of composition does involve planning.

CRACK-THE-CODE

Crack-the-Code was developed from Das and Heemsbergen's (1983) work on planning, simultaneous, and successive cognitive processes.

Their investigation showed that the game *Mastermind* involved considerable planning processes. Crack-the-Code has certain similarities with this game but is designed to be more efficient in terms of administration time and materials needed.

Crack-the-Code (see Figure 6.1) requires the subject to determine the correct sequence of colored chips when given only a limited amount of information by the experimenter. The full version of the task has 16 items. In the first item, one instruction line and two chips of the same color are used. The number of both is then increased step-by-step so that in the last item, five instruction lines and five chips of different colors are used. Next to each instruction line is one of the following statements: "none correct", "one correct", "two correct", or "three correct". This provides the subject with information that none, one, two, or three of the colors on a particular line appear in the correct serial location. To arrive at the correct answer, the subject must analyze the problem, extract relevant information, develop and evaluate possible solutions, and modify the generated solutions if necessary. The subject is usually given one trial to determine the correct order of chips for each item and the time limit for each item is three minutes. The task is interrupted after two consecutive failures and the subject's score is the number of correctly solved items (accuracy score). Also, the time score can be used to detect individual differences in performance speed. Figure 6.1 displays a black and white version of a medium difficulty item.

Three different versions of the task have been used. In the standard version, instruction lines contain colored chips and the subject is given similar chips that s/he must place in the correct order on the answer line. The paper and pencil versions of the task use either round patterns with the color name in the middle (as shown above) or different symbols (for example, circle, cross, box, etc.). Instead of using manipulable objects, the subject is asked to write the correct answer on the answer line. The third version of the task is a fully computerized application of the standard version. In this version, the subject drags the colored chips to their correct location by using a mouse and the computer records the entire protocol and provides time and accuracy scores.

We believe that because of its complexity, Crack-the-Code relies specifically on such late developing abilities as forming and remembering multistep plans, allocating attention to the most relevant

Table 6.1
The Planned Composition Rating Scale

EXPRESSION	1	2	3	4	5	6	7
	Appears that thought has been given to the story; writer says what is meant; points related to the topic; no padding.			Impression given that the writer does not fully understand what is meant; does not relate clearly; some padding and irrelevant material.			Hard to tell what the writer is saying; makes little sense; gives the impression of trying to get something on paper.

ORGANIZATION	1	2	3	4	5	6	7
	Good starting point; has a sense of directed movement in story; appears to have an underlying plan; seems logically arranged.			Organization is standard and conventional; some trivial points given more importance than deserved; logic in progression is not always clear.			Starts anywhere and never gets anywhere; ideas are presented randomly with no apparent forethought.

WORDING	1	2	3	4	5	6	7
	Use of uncommon words or words in unusual combinations which shows imagination; word experiments need not be successful 100% of time.			Uses common phrases or expressions; no apparent concern with the use of words.			Uses words carelessly; many mistakes in usage; unclear wording or childish vocabulary.

MECHANICS

1	2	3	4	5	6	7
No serious errors in sentence structure; punctuation correct; spelling consistent & appropriate for grade.			Some errors in structure but does not obscure meaning, violations in punctuation and spelling.			Serious errors in sentence structure making story difficult to understand; many punctuation errors make story fragmented; many spelling mistakes.

INDIVIDUALITY

1	2	3	4	5	6	7
Unique or creative approach to material; unusual or original ideas; gives story a "twist".			Some originality shown; few interesting or unique aspects.			Not original at all; ideas are mundane, not creative and uninteresting.

Figure 6.1
An Example of a Crack-the-Code item

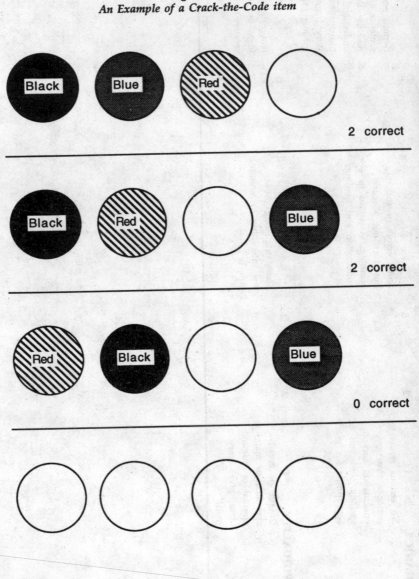

features of the task, and successive refinement of one's hypotheses. Thus, it should be a good indicator of individual differences in planning skills during the school years and adulthood.

The remainder of this chapter will be divided into three parts. The first part will include a discussion of the role of speed and working memory in conceptual planning. In the second part, we will present several studies that have used Crack-the-Code and Planned Composition to study planning in writing and managerial decision making. Finally, the third part will include a discussion of the use of verbal protocols for monitoring strategies while subjects are completing Crack-the-Code. The importance of such online data for understanding the development and structure of planning processes will also be emphasized.

CONCEPTUAL PLANNING, SPEED, AND WORKING MEMORY

We need to separate speed from accuracy in many of the planning tasks. Whereas tasks such as Visual Search appear to depend entirely on speed, other tasks such as Matching Numbers and Crack-the-Code appear to involve greater contributions from working memory. Thus, we must consider the processes that determine speed of response and separate these processes from those that are contributed to by working memory.

In fact, the entire notion of speed should be reviewed. Since performance is usually measured either by a speed or accuracy score, we believe that speed should not be singled out as a unique measure of *intellectual functions* separate from accuracy with respect to the underlying processes that the tasks may require for their solution. In other words, one cannot build a theory of cognitive processes solely on the basis of speed, as some researchers, including Jensen (1987), have done. We know that there is a tradeoff between speed and accuracy. Several studies have indicated that in many tasks, speed can be substituted for accuracy and vice versa (Shiffrin and Schneider, 1977). So, what is speed, then? What we may in fact be measuring in speed is the speed of encoding for simple tasks (for example, reaction time) where accuracy scores exhibit little variance. In other words, the task is so easy that individual differences in performance reflect speed rather than accuracy. In this way, speed of performance in Crack-the-Code may reflect encoding time, especially with easy items. Working memory may determine performance (measured in terms of accuracy) in some, but not all, planning tasks, as discussed below. To use an example from the planning tasks that we have used, consider automatic visual search. Here the subject is required to detect a picture among numbers; it can only be measured in terms of speed as the task is extremely simple. Nevertheless, the detection of a picture among numbers is faster than its opposite—namely, the detection of a number among pictures. The latter probably reflects a higher level of complexity. The second task therefore involves the operation of strategic search but working memory capacity does not influence performance differences. In neither automatic search nor in controlled search does working memory play an important role. In contrast, in a task such as Matching Numbers (especially when the length of the list of numbers exceeds four), working memory begins to play an important role. These longer lists, which are above the span for primary memory, require the resources of rehearsal and other mechanisms. Here, speed becomes relatively unimportant unless the individual is extremely slow in encoding the digits, with the result that little capacity is left in working memory for continuing with the Matching Numbers task.

A task such as Crack-the-Code has both simple and complex items. The simple items may be sensitive to differences in speed, whereas the complex items probably are not. Similarly, the simple tasks would not be influenced significantly by working memory, whereas the complex tasks would be. An alternative hypothesis would be to expect just the opposite, namely, that in simple tasks, speed would not be a sensitive measure of individual differences. In complex tasks, however, it would be an important variable. At a later point in this chapter, we will attempt to determine which of these hypotheses is correct.

SPEED AND WORKING MEMORY: NEUROPSYCHOLOGICAL CONSIDERATIONS

The following observations on *neuropsychological aspects* of speed and working memory are made as part of the background for interpreting the results concerning how memory and speed can influence Crack-the-Code performance. Speed, as measured by automatic Visual Search, can be regarded as a function of the lower cortical area and the limbic system. It is perhaps not unjustified to consider speed of this variety to be the same as reaction time and essentially a process related to attention. Reaction time, inspection time, and similar measures of speed can reflect the time required to encode simple stimuli. It is therefore reasonable to assume that the speed of encoding is dependent upon alertness and the efficiency of the orienting response, both of which are concepts within the attention–arousal component of the PASS theory.

Working memory, on the other hand, is located in both the frontal lobes and (for verbal material) the area adjacent to the temporal lobe. Working memory can be a strategy-dependent function because its efficiency depends on the parsimonious use of a limited memory capacity as well as executive mechanisms such as rehearsal, which maintain items in working memory until recall is required. In this respect, working memory requires the mobilization of attentional resources and memory-related strategies. Rehearsal and other strategic components are probably more closely associated with the frontal and frontal–temporal areas, whereas memory for order can be conceived of as being more a function of the temporal lobe than of the frontal lobe. Thus, both conceptually and neuropsychologically, speed and working memory can be distinguished to a certain extent but not entirely. Tasks such as Visual Search in the automatic format primarily measure speed and can be included within the attention–arousal component of the PASS theory. In contrast, controlled search is clearly a frontal lobe function. But does it overlap with the region that is associated with the working memory function? If it does, then it may provide a strong basis for recognizing a clear distinction between speed and working memory. At the present time, however, we do not appear to have any strong evidence that the two can be separated.

How Memory and Speed Influence Planning?: Experiments with Crack-the-Code

A study done in Finland by Parrila, Äystö, and Das (1994) focused on the relationship between planning and other PASS components but also produced information about the relationship between working memory and Crack-the-Code. Several planning tasks, including Crack-the-Code, were given to grades 2, 4, and 11 students, together with six tests assessing attention, simultaneous, and successive processing. Factor analysis of these six tests produced a successive factor that was defined by three working memory tasks: Number Recall, Word Recall, and Figure Memory. (The last test had a minor loading of .4 on the successive factor, compared to its loading of .7 on the simultaneous factor.) When the effect of age was partialled out, the correlation between accuracy score on Crack-the-Code and successive factor score was reduced to insignificance. Furthermore, regression analysis within grade levels showed that Crack-the-Code score was not predicted significantly by successive factor score for any of the grade levels. The authors concluded that memory span does not explain subjects' performance on this task; instead, the need for a strategic approach is the dominant feature.

The second, more comprehensive, study on this topic was conducted by Kar and Misra in order to examine the relative contribution of working memory and speed to both Crack-the-Code outcomes: solution time and accuracy of performance.

Subjects were 70 college students from two towns in India. Aside from Crack-the-Code, they were given other tests of CAS (Cognitive Assessment System), which will be described as we consider the working memory and speed components. In order to produce a working memory score, two successive processing variables, the Sentence Repetition score and the Serial Order Memory score from the Word Series test, were combined. The range of scores on both variables was then divided at the median. The High Working Memory group consisted of subjects who scored above the median on both variables and the Low Working Memory group consisted of those subjects who scored below the median on both. The remainder of the subjects were classified as the Middle Working Memory group.

In terms of the relationship between working memory and speed or accuracy of solving Crack-the-Code problems, analysis of variance indicated that those with high accuracy scores on Crack-the-Code also tended to have high scores on working memory. The correlations between working memory and Crack-the-Code scores were less informative in that working memory scores were significantly correlated with both speed and accuracy of solving Crack-the-Code items. This may imply that working memory scores reflected a general cognitive competence. Thus, the most meaningful finding was that the ability to solve Crack-the-Code problems, especially at medium difficulty levels, was positively related to working memory capacity as derived from Sentence Repetition and Word Series tests.

A general speed score was obtained next. Word Reading (words in black type on a white surface) and Color Naming time, which were obtained from the Stroop test, were first combined to form a single speed score. The Automatic Visual Search time formed the other speed score. Those with high scores on both tests were then compared to those with low scores on both tests in terms of their performance on the Crack-the-Code task.

If a general speed factor exists, then significant group differences should be present in the speed of solution for Crack-the-Code items. This was found to be true in terms of the time required to solve Crack-the-Code items of medium and high difficulty. Another significant finding was that the general speed score was not related to accuracy of performance on Crack-the-Code, implying that if one is fast according to both speed tests (i.e., Stroop and Automatic Search), one is not necessarily more or less accurate in solving Crack-the-Code problems. These results make intuitive sense: a general speed factor does significantly affect the speed of solution for Crack-the-Code problems of medium and high difficulty but it does not relate to accuracy of performance.

These results may also have broader implications. For example, if we suspect that an individual is slow because of age or a slow general tempo, s/he will not necessarily be poor at solving a complex planning problem such as the one exemplified in Crack-the-Code. Alternatively, if an individual is poor in working memory, s/he is likely to be relatively less competent in solving Crack-the-Code problems of medium difficulty. Items of high difficulty had so little variance in the accuracy score (i.e., most of the subjects did not pass these items) that we were unable to reach any conclusion about the involvement of working memory in them. It would, however, be reasonable to expect that with a better-performing sample, the correlation between working memory and difficult Crack-the-Code items would also be significant.

PLANNING IN WRITING AND
MANAGERIAL DECISION MAKING

NARRATIVE COMPOSITION AND INDIVIDUAL
DIFFERENCES IN PLANNING

The planning and organizational difficulties exhibited by poor writers have been clearly recognized (Newcomer and Barenbaum, 1991). This could explain why children who are poor at writing do not necessarily improve even when taught directly by their teachers. Ashman and Das (1980) have shown that lack of planning in compositions can be related to deficiencies in simple planning tasks such as Visual Search and Trail Making. Poor writers are poor in cognitive tasks involving planning but is there a causal link? The next question would involve whether or not a certain degree of competency in cognitive planning is required before an individual can begin to apply this skill to organize information in a composition. Is there a threshold in the planning–writing relationship?

A study by Mishra (1992) sought to investigate these questions. Specifically, he was interested in determining if good writers are better than poor writers in cognitive tests of planning, as well as in their use of organizational skills in written composition. A second question focused on whether the relationship between planning and writing is marked only above a certain level of writing competency.

Subjects were Canadian school children (48 boys and 59 girls) from regular grade 8 classes and their mean age was 14 years. A Test of Written Language (TOWL-2; Hammill and Larsen, 1988) was administered to subjects in groups, with the help of teachers. Planned Composition (Ashman and Das, 1980) and three planning tests (i.e., Planned Codes, Planned Connections, and Matching Numbers) from the Planning Battery of the Cognitive Assessment System (Das and Naglieri, 1993) were administered. Teachers provided ratings of students' writing skills on a 7-point scale, with "one" representing "very poor" and "seven" representing "very superior".

The results were analyzed in several ways. First, based on their performance on the TOWL-2, the upper and lower 30 percent of the total sample were designated as good and poor writers, respectively. One-way multivariate analyses of variance were performed to compare these two groups on planning tasks and on Planned

Composition variables. The results indicated that good writers performed significantly better than poor writers on all three planning tasks. Good writers were also significantly better than poor writers on all Planned Composition variables such as Expression, Organization, Wording, Mechanics, and Individuality. Moreover, the Organization variable related best to Planning. It may therefore be reasonable to assume that good writers are not only better than poor writers on cognitive tests of planning but also in their use of planning and organizational skills in writing.

The relationship between planning and writing for good and poor writers was examined separately for children of average intelligence (i.e., IQs of 90 to 112). Cognitive planning was found to be related to writing for good writers but not for poor writers, supporting the assumption that a certain level of competency in cognitive planning may be required to evidence its application in writing. This hypothesis was further tested in a linear structural relationship model (LISREL), where it was expected that competency in cognitive planning would influence Planned Composition score and that Planned Composition score would, in turn, influence writing performance. As expected, the data for the entire sample displayed a good fit for this model: the path from cognitive planning to Planned Composition was .214 and the path from Planned Composition to writing was .504. Thus, as we move from a low to a high score on cognitive planning, we can begin to see its influence, first, on Planned Composition and, second, on writing performance in general.

PLANNING AND MANAGERIAL DECISION MAKING

The ability to find parsimonious solutions to problems and to make good judgements and decisions is part of the core competence of management executives. We know that top-level executives have to plan, set goals, solve problems, and make decisions, and all of these are often performed under poorly structured and uncertain conditions. It is no surprise, then, that managers differ in the quality of the decisions that they make. But what accounts for these differences? The two main explanations involve motivational predisposition and cognitive competence (Das, Misra, & Mishra, 1993). In this section, we will concentrate on cognitive competence.

Despite the apparently obvious conclusion that success in complex occupations should be related to intelligence, there is only mixed evidence that intelligence tests are predictive of occupational success (Sen & Das, 1991). This assumes, however, that intelligence is defined according to traditional tests such as the Wechsler series. These tests are limited because they are mainly measures of simultaneous and (to a lesser extent) successive processes, and do not measure planning or attentional processes. Planning processes are especially important when prediction of managerial success is at issue because planning processes are related to complex tasks (Das, Naglieri, & Kirby, 1994) and also to factors that are sometimes described as personality attributes—persistence, motivation, independence, cooperation, and flexibility. The following two studies illustrate the relationship between planning processes and performance in a managerial task and in a demanding managerial job within the banking industry.

The Strategic Planning Test

The first study used a specifically designed strategic planning test. In this test, the individual is asked to write a composition, taking into account cursory notes as well as four company objectives for maximizing profit (see Table 6.2).

This study was done in collaboration with S. Misra in India (Das et al., 1993). Subjects for the study were 157 postgraduate students in one of the leading institutes for management in India (i.e., Indian Institute of Management, Ahmedabad). We expected that in such a homogeneous group the range of individual differences would be small. Students were asked to write a one- to two-page essay, taking into account the four strategies for the company to prosper. Essays were rated by three judges using the rating scale displayed in Table 6.3.

Scores from different items were then subjected to a factor analysis. For the purpose of factor analysis, similar items were combined as follows: Items 1 and 2 were combined, giving one score, and items 5, 6, 7, and 8 were combined, giving a competency score. Thus, the factor analysis was carried out on six items. The results of the factor analysis are reported in Table 6.4.

Two factors were obtained. Although there were split loadings for some of the items, a clear pattern appears to have emerged.

Table 6.2
A Test of Strategic Planning

Phase I:

Suppose, in a pharmaceutical company, you are the Chief Executive Officer. The company can have the following overall strategies in order to prosper:

- A   be innovative
- B   achieve a good share of the market
- C   be known for its economical price—low cost of products
- D   produce high quality goods.

Cautionary Notes for Each Strategy

'A' requires on outlay of capital in research and development. But the world record shows that in the last five years, research and development money has increased five-fold, but the number of new products launched has remained the same. 'B' requires aggressive advertisement, but the company's star product (i.e., Bayer Aspirin) is about to be replaced by a new breakthrough medication for fever. 'C' requires getting the components of the products from manufacturing to packaging from developing countries where labor is cheap. But this has a disastrous effect on employment at home. 'D' may cost so much more that it would make the product uneconomical.

In the 30-year past history of the company, the following weight had been given to the strategies with results indicated. Your job is to achieve a 100 percent growth by rearranging the strategies, but you must take into account the information from the past results:

In the past, one manager gave 1st place to C, 2nd place to D, 3rd place to A, and 4th place to B. None of CDAB was in the correct position. Again, we do not know which ones these were. The profit again was 50 percent because like the previous choice, only two of the strategies were in the correct place. BCDA=2.

Your task is to assign the priorities so that the right strategy will have the right place to give a 100 percent profit.

Phase II:

Write an essay of about one page justifying how the plan produces the best results when the solution is DCBA (or BADC).

Table 6.3

The Assessment System for Strategic Essays

1. Have all the strategic choices been mentioned in the essay?

1	2	3	4	5	6	7
Mentions all 4 strategies clearly		Mentions all 2 to 3 strategies clearly			Does not mention any of the strategies	

2. Has justification been given for the relative positions of the strategies?

1	2	3	4	5	6	7
Justification for all 4 strategies provided clearly		Justification for 2 to 3 strategies provided clearly			Does not provide justification for the relative positions of the strategies	

3. Have the cautionary notes been used directly or indirectly?

1	2	3	4	5	6	7
All 4 cautionary notes are used directly or indirectly		Two or three cautionary notes are used directly or indirectly			None of the cautionary notes are used directly or indirectly	

4. Is there evidence of external knowledge?

1	2	3	4	5	6	7
Extensive use of information not included in the description provided for the task		Some utilization of information not included in the description provided for the task			No utilization of information not included in the description provided for the task	

5. Have conjunctives, qualifiers (even, although, etc.), conditionals (if, since, except, etc.), and causalities (because, so, therefore, hence, etc.) been used appropriately?

1	2	3	4	5	6	7
All conjunctives are used in a logical and meaningful manner		Some confusion in the use of conjunctives			Most conjunctives are used inappropriately	

6. Do sentences follow one another logically and meaningfully?

1	2	3	4	5	6	7
All sentences flow logically and meaningfully		Some sentences do not flow logically and meaningfully			Many sentences do not flow logically and meaningfully	

7. Do paragraphs have distinct themes?

1	2	3	4	5	6	7
Specific themes are clearly expressed in each paragraph		Some paragraphs have unclear/overlapping/disjointed themes			Most paragraphs have unclear/overlapping/disjointed themes	

8. Do paragraphs follow one another logically and meaningfully?

1	2	3	4	5	6	7
All paragraphs flow logically and meaningfully from one another with necessary transitional statements		Some paragraphs do not flow logically and meaningfully from one another. Some deficiencies in making a transition			Most paragraphs do not flow logically and meaningfully from one another. Inappropriate transitions	

9. Is there a structure in the composition?

1	2	3	4	5	6	7

Good starting point, ideas are presented concisely, has a sense of direction in the composition leading to a definite conclusion

Has an overall sense of direction. Some inconsistency and redundancy

Lacks starting point. Never gets anywhere. Full of conflicting and inconsistent and irrelevant ideas.

10. Is the composition unique/original?

1	2	3	4	5	6	7

Unique and creative approach to material. Unusual or original ideas give the composition a "twist"

Some originality shown. Few interesting or unique aspects

Not original at all. Ideas are mundane, not creative and uninteresting

Table 6.4

Principal Components Orthogonal Solution–Varimax for Six Derived Items of the Strategic Planning Test

Items	Factor I	Factor II	h^2
Mean of Items 1 & 2	.86	.33	.85
Item 3	.55	.62	.69
Item 4	.27	.93	.93
Mean of Items 5, 6, 7, 8	.82	.36	.80
Item 9	.86	.37	.88
Item 10	.46	.82	.88
Percentage Variance	73.5	10.5	

Note: h^2 = communality estimate.

We were able to identify the first factor by the items that measure internal organization. In other words, it is a factor score indicating organizational skills that are dependent on the composition skills exhibited in the essay itself. In contrast, the second factor can be labeled as external organization: items 4 and 10, which have the highest loadings on this factor, use outside knowledge beyond the content of the essay. We believe that internal and external organization are somewhat similar to the concepts of horizontal and lateral thinking suggested by de Bono (1986).

Selecting Management Executives: Planning and Performance on a Complex Job

The second managerial planning study (Das and Naglieri, 1993), explored the relationship between planning and job performance within the investment banking sector. Das and Naglieri focused on a position, quantitative analyst, within the research area of a major investment bank. The person in this position is required to analyze the portfolios of a bank's financial holdings to assess the quality of the investments, predict the rate of return over various time intervals, and recommend alternative investment configurations to obtain the desired level of return. This job requires various attributes such as motivation, organization, analytical thinking, and good interpersonal skills. According to the supervisors of these quantitative analysts, the following are seen as particularly important:

- The ability to define and analyze a problem.
- Pooling knowledge to solve problems.
- The ability to understand work.
- Persistence when performing a difficult task.
- Good organization and planning skills.
- Knowing what decisions can be made independently.
- Knowing when to seek information or the help of others.
- Flexibility and receptiveness to other ideas.
- Adaptability to the ambiguities of the task.

These activities certainly involve planning. Both planning and the task of the quantitative analyst require organization, hypothesis generation, problem solving, self-monitoring, and completing tasks efficiently. Because the intellectual requirements of the quantitative analyst's job are consistent with the construct of planning as described in this book, a complex planning test for adults like Crack-the-Code should be effective in predicting high or low job performance.

To examine the extent to which Crack-the-Code would be effective in identifying individuals whose job performance would be highly or poorly rated by their supervisors, 30 subjects (16 males and 14 females) were used. These individuals were current employees at one of the largest investment banks in the world, located on Wall Street. Subjects were selected by managers so that a range of competence on the job would be represented. All subjects had been working as quantitative analysts for at least one year.

Subjects' job performance was rated by their supervisors using a brief rating scale developed from job descriptors. The Brief Evaluation of Activity Form (BEAF) was constructed to provide a rating of activities considered important by upper management (e.g., understanding a problem, being aware of the goals to be attained, selecting the best approach, seeing alternatives, minimizing risks, thinking critically, etc.). The items included in this form are displayed in Table 6.5.

The Crack-the-Code task was administered in groups and each subject's score was the number of items answered correctly within a 45-minute time limit. Upper managers responsible for supervising the quantitative analysts completed the BEAF for each individual that they supervised. Each subject's item scores were summarized

Table 6.5
The Brief Evaluation of Activity Form

Instructions: When faced with many complex tasks to complete, employees can behave in various ways. This form is used to rate the individual on the following items about work performance. Please use a 3 point scale: **1 for Always; 2 for Sometimes; 3 for Seldom**. Rate the individual based on how often he or she acts in the ways described.

How often does the employee...	Always	Some-times	Seldom
1. understand what is required?	1	2	3
2. is unaware of what problems are to be avoided?	1	2	3
3. is clearly aware of what goals are to be attained?	1	2	3
4. knows what seems to be the best approach to take?	1	2	3
5. neglects asking what previous information can be retrieved?	1	2	3
6. knows what new information should be obtained?	1	2	3
7. goes beyond the minimal requirement?	1	2	3
8. ignores other alternatives?	1	2	3
9. considers what other information might aid in the solution of the problem?	1	2	3
10. is unaware of the pros and cons for each alternative?	1	2	3
11. knows which alternatives appear to be the best?	1	2	3
12. knows how to minimize risks?	1	2	3
13. cannot develop alternative plans?	1	2	3
14. can monitor the steps taken to solve a problem?	1	2	3
15. thinks critically about what has been produced?	1	2	3
16. accepts information about the drawbacks of his/her solution?	1	2	3

© *Copyright by J. P. Das and J. A. Naglieri*

to yield a total raw score, which was then transformed into a standard score.

Internal reliability was .981 for the BEAF and .895 for Crack-the-Code, using the split-half method (corrected using the Spearman–Brown formula). The relationships between the planning test, Crack-the-Code, and the evaluation of actual job performance as determined by the BEAF were examined in several ways. First, the rankings of individuals on the basis of their BEAF and Crack-the-Code scores were correlated. The coefficient (Spearman Rho = .553) was significant.

Next, the average BEAF rating scores were compared for subjects who scored highest and lowest on the Crack-the-Code task. The group with the lowest Crack-the-Code scores earned a mean BEAF score of 89.1 and those with the highest Crack-the-Code scores earned a mean BEAF score of 111.8. The difference between these means was significant.

Finally, the BEAF scores for subjects who scored highest and for subjects who scored lowest on Crack-the-Code were contrasted. The difference in BEAF scores was significant, indicating that Crack-the-Code was effective in identifying those who were rated as good and those who were rated as poor in job performance on the basis of the BEAF rating scales.

The results of this study suggest that planning, a construct not measured by traditional IQ tests, is related to job performance in a demanding employment setting. More specifically, planning as a process appears to be related to complex job performance involving organization, defining a problem, independent functioning, flexibility, and adaptation.

The Connection Between Crack-the-Code and Planned Composition

The three previous studies focused on either Crack-the-Code or Planned Composition as measured by the Strategic Planning test. The connection between the tasks was the focus of the next study. If both tasks are indeed predictive of subjects' performance, then the question emerges: Is there a common planning component for both Crack-the-Code and strategic Planned Composition? This question was investigated by Mathur and Das (1994) using undergraduate and graduate engineering students from the Indian Institute of Technology.

Thirty-three subjects completed the Crack-the-Code test and wrote a composition following the same procedure outlined in Das et al. (1993). Crack-the-Code was administered under standard conditions, except that items were projected onto a screen and subjects were given a maximum of 2 minutes to solve the easier items and a maximum of 3 minutes to solve the more difficult items. In scoring Crack-the-Code, items were divided into three categories: hard, medium, and easy. The easy items did not display any variance; all subjects were able to do them correctly.

Scoring the composition followed the procedure described in the Das et al. (1993) study and produced a total composition score, an internal organization score, and an external organization score. The latter two scores were formed according to the factor structure found by Das et al.

The correlation (.433) between the total accuracy score on Crack-the-Code and the total composition score was significant. In other words, the two variables shared approximately 20 percent of the variance. Correlations between the internal organization score and the external organization score with the total Crack-the-Code score were in the same range. Also, correlations between both medium difficulty and difficult Crack-the-Code items with external organization score were of the same magnitude and statistically significant. Thus, there is no doubt that one score could be predicted to a certain extent from the other score but let us now examine whether Crack-the-Code is a better predictor of Composition or vice versa.

The sample was divided into three groups (low, medium, high) first on the basis of their composition performance and then on the basis of their Crack-the-Code accuracy score. Subsequent ANOVAs showed significant differences between the groups in composition scores when the division was based on Crack-the-Code items of medium difficulty but not when difficult Crack-the-Code items were used. The difficult items were too difficult for most of the subjects and the range of scores was therefore restricted, which probably explains why the ANOVA was nonsignificant.

Post hoc Scheffé tests showed that the group that was poorest in medium difficulty Crack-the-Code items also had significantly poorer internal and total composition scores than the other two groups. Thus, medium difficulty Crack-the-Code items seem to be effective in identifying those who are also poor in composition.

When subjects were assigned to one of three groups on the basis of their composition scores (using internal organization score as the basis for this division), a significant group effect was found in their Crack-the-Code performance. Again, the high- and middle-scoring groups differed from the low-scoring group but only on items of medium difficulty. Furthermore, the means for the total Crack-the-Code score for groups scoring high or low on total composition were significantly different.

We believe that these detailed analyses using ANOVA confirm the positive correlation between Crack-the-Code performance and strategic planning, and add specific information about their relationship to one another. Assigning subjects to groups on the basis of their Crack-the-Code performance, particularly when items of medium difficulty were used, allowed us to better predict subjects' performance on composition than did assigning subjects to groups on the basis of composition scores and attempting to predict their performance on Crack-the-Code.

In sum, it is remarkable that accuracy in performance on a complex planning task, Crack-the-Code, can predict students' ability to write coherent, integrated essays in which they were required to consider all four company objectives as well as cautionary notes for supporting each objective. In rating these essays, raters looked mainly at causal links between sentences and between sentences and paragraphs. Rating compositions in this manner, however, is not an entirely objective method. Yet, it is encouraging that the ratings of compositions could be predicted by an entirely objective test performance.

VERBAL PROTOCOLS AND INDIVIDUAL DIFFERENCES IN PLANNING

Verbal protocols that subjects produce while they are solving a problem provide an opportunity for researchers to discover what subjects are thinking (Ericsson and Simon, 1993) and how the process of planning unfolds during performance. Thus, verbal protocols can provide us with detailed information about individual differences in the process of planning, especially in more complex tasks such as Crack-the-Code or Planned Composition. Before introducing a recent study that involved collecting verbal protocols during the Crack-the-Code task, we will briefly discuss the think aloud method.

THE THINK ALOUD METHOD

Ericsson and Simon (1980, 1993), perhaps the best known proponents of this approach, suggest that the think aloud method can be used to gain reliable information about subjects' internal cognitive processes:

> With this procedure, the heeded information may be verbalized either through direct articulation or by verbal encoding of information that was originally stored in a nonverbal code. With the instruction to verbalize, a direct trace is obtained of the heeded information, and hence, an indirect one of the internal stages of the cognitive process (Ericsson & Simon, 1980, p. 220).

Ericsson and Simon have also developed an information-processing theory of the cognitive processes involved in thinking aloud. To summarize, the theory establishes a link between a central processor (CP), sensory memories, and long-term (LTM) and short-term memories (STM). CP, which regulates all nonautomatic cognitive processes, decides what part of the information available in sensory memories and in LTM will be placed in STM. When verbalizing, subjects only have access to information in STM and the verbal protocol will therefore consist of some portion of that information.

If the information in STM is represented in verbal form, then verbalizing this information is possible without making additional demands on STM or the CP. If information in STM is not verbally represented, then verbalization requires first making corresponding verbal representations (for example, giving names or labels to the visually presented objects). When this is done, some information that was present in STM may not be verbalized due to the demands that recoding makes on processing capacity and processing time. If further demands are made of the CP, verbalization will provide an even less complete account of solution processes.

Moreover, Ericsson and Simon (1980, p. 219) distinguished between several levels of verbalization that relate to processing demands: "When information is reproduced in the form in which it was acquired from the central processor, we will speak of *direct* or *Level 1* verbalization. When one or more mediating processes occur between attention to the information and its delivery, we will speak of *encoded Level 2* or *Level 3* verbalization". In direct verbalization, the subject verbalizes only those thoughts that come to her or his mind during the task solution without trying to explain or reflect upon them. It is also assumed that most of these thoughts will be readily accessible in verbal form, perhaps in the form of verbal inner speech. At Level 2, information is not initially represented verbally and the subject must first translate it into verbal form before verbalization can take place. At Level 3, the subject is required to go beyond simply talking aloud and, for example, attend to specific information or to explain his or her thoughts to the experimenter.

The level of verbalization that the subject will be engaged in can be influenced by the type of instructions s/he is given. The instructions "talk out loud while solving the problem" can produce a very different response than the directive "explain what you are thinking about". Levels of verbalization can also be influenced by the characteristics of the task to be performed. If the task contains material that is not readily verbally codeable, then it is likely that the subject will be involved in Level 2 rather than Level 1 verbalizing.

Lawson and Rice (1987) distinguished between three types of verbalization: introspective, concurrent, and retrospective. Introspective and retrospective verbalization are reports on what has happened after the subject has had time to reflect upon his or her thoughts. Moreover, they do not necessarily reflect the actual process that the subject was engaged in while solving the problem (Ericsson and Simon, 1993). Concurrent verbalization involves Level 1 and Level 2 verbalization, and requires the subject to verbalize his or her thoughts at the time that s/he is working through a problem. According to Ericsson and Simon (1993), concurrent verbalization produces valid data on subjects' cognitive processes given that certain guidelines (i.e., type and length of task, instructions and training) are followed. For the purpose of studying planning processes during Crack-the-Code or Planned Composition, concurrent verbalization seems valuable since it provides a running record of what the subject is thinking about and attending to, and this data is not marred by changes that the subject may make after having had time to think more about the task. For this reason, the following study of the development of planning involved the collection and analysis of concurrent verbal protocols.

THE DEVELOPMENT OF PLANNING AND THINK ALOUD

One specific question that verbal protocols can answer better than more traditional quantitative measures such as speed of responding and accuracy of the solution is *how* children plan and solve problems at different ages. A recent study by Parrila and Papadopoulos (1994) addressed this question by collecting verbal protocols for the Crack-the-Code task. As we saw in Chapter 4, existing studies of planning development provide information about some of the abilities that may develop but they generally do not answer the question of how children plan and solve problems at different ages. In other words, they yield quantitative data about general trends and group averages but they do not provide us with data about how individual children succeed or fail in their attempts and how the process of solving a problem or formulating a plan develops.

The main objective of this study was therefore to observe whether we could identify both general trends and individual differences in children's planning for two grade levels using the Crack-the-Code task and the think aloud method. The sample consisted of 8 students, 4 of which were from each of the two grade levels (i.e., grades 4 and 8). Three items from Crack-the-Code were used: item A required subjects to put three colors in the correct order, taking into account two instruction lines; and items B and C required subjects to arrange four colors in the correct order, taking into account information from three instruction lines. The maximum performance time allowed for each item was 180 seconds. Performance time and accuracy of solution (i.e., pass/fail) was recorded for all subjects and provided the quantitative measures (product data). Verbal protocols, in turn, provided the qualitative, or procedural, data.

The three Crack-the-Code items were analyzed prior to data collection and a set of hypothetical solution models was developed for each of them. Four hypothetical solution models or search strategies were constructed. They were:

1. *Random Search,* which is essentially the same as a trial and error method;
2. *Climbing,* in which the subject attempts to place one color at a time in its position or proceeds one position at a time trying to find the correct color for the position;
3. *Pattern,* in which the subject builds the solution as a response to one instruction line; and
4. *Combination,* in which the subject integrates information from two or three instruction lines when building hypotheses about the correct answer (for example, comparing line 1 with line 2).

These hypothetical solution models were all represented in subjects' performance. Several protocols included statements indicating more than one solution model since the subject changed the search strategy used during the task. Table 6.6 provides short examples of how subjects' verbal protocols displayed Climbing, Pattern, and Combination strategies.

In addition, all protocols were checked for the presence of (*a*) definition of the Search Space at the beginning of the task, (*b*) evaluation of the correctness of the answer, (*c*) confusion, and

Table 6.6
*Three Examples of the Subjects' Protocols
Displaying Different Search Strategies*

---

1. Climbing
Grade 4 subject, Item A:
   - if the Blue one isn't in the beginning of these ones, it would probably be at the beginning of that one
   - and the same with Black
   - and the White is not here, so it should go there . . .

2. Pattern
Grade 8 subject, Item B:
   - 2 correct (Line 1; has already put White on correct position)
   - so Black (second correct)
   - we could switch blue and red around . . .

3. Combination
Grade 8 subject, Item C:
   - Okay, if there's blue and white here and they say that none of them are correct,
   - then here where there are 2 correct, Blue and White can't be . . .

(*d*) application failures, which were diagnosed if a subject who verbalized a functional strategy failed to implement it properly.

The results of the study indicated that item A was too easy for subjects and did not produce any differences in procedure or product measures. It is therefore not discussed here.

Items B and C both produced rich procedural data about how different subjects approached these items and what, if anything, may have gone wrong. Verbal protocols from items B and C allowed us to detect variability both within a single performance as well as between groups of subjects. For example, grade 4 subjects expressed a considerable amount of confusion about item B and none of them defined the Search Space at the beginning of the item. Also, the two subjects who passed the item used vastly different strategies (i.e., Random Search versus Combination). In contrast, grade 8 subjects tended to use more complex strategies, define the Search Space, and evaluate their answers more often than younger subjects. None of them indicated confusion. Thus, analysis of verbal protocols from item B showed that grade 8 subjects were clearly more advanced in their planning; in fact, their performance in general was quite well rounded, with all the necessary components present.

Protocols from item C showed that only one grade 4 subject was capable of using a functional strategy for this item, whereas the others approached the item in a random manner. None of these subjects defined the Search Space and only one subject evaluated the answer. In contrast, all but one grade 8 subject defined the Search Space and used at least a Pattern strategy. It is interesting to note that although two grade 8 subjects used a Combination strategy, neither of them passed the item: one managed to build only a partial plan, whereas the other failed to apply a functional plan. In sum, it seems that grade 8 subjects approached this item in a more strategic manner (i.e., using more defining and evaluation) than grade 4 subjects. This did not, however, lead to a better end result: the only grade 8 subject who passed this item used Random Search and guessed the correct answer.

These findings gain more importance as valid and efficient measures of planning when compared with the outcomes of product measures. Results from product measures for items B and C can be summarized briefly as follows: Grade 4 subjects (*a*) completed the items as successfully as grade 8 subjects and (*b*) were slightly faster than their older counterparts (the time difference was significant for item C because of a ceiling effect). This leads us to conclude that had we collected data only on the product measures, conclusions about grade differences would have been rather different than what the protocol data suggested. For example, if teaching decisions were based on product measures, then all children could essentially be taught the same things and in the same manner, since these measures indicated no differences in children's performance.

Longer versions of Crack-the-Code (i.e., more items of the same difficulty) should also be useful for studying microgenetic change (i.e., how a student learns a principle for solving a problem within one session) and the role of variability in this process. If, for example, within-subject variability proves to be as important a factor for learning and development as Siegler (1994) suggests, then methods that do not tend to conceal this variability are certainly needed in order to develop effective interventions.

Results from this study clearly suggest that collecting verbal protocols during the Crack-the-Code task is a useful way to identify both general trends and individual differences in planning development. Moreover, verbal protocols help us to detect both within- and between-group variability, as well as intra-individual variability in planning that could not be detected with product measures. There are very few planning tasks currently available that can be used to assess individual differences in adolescence and beyond. We would like to suggest Crack-the-Code as having potential in this regard.

Furthermore, verbal protocols also indicate whether subjects are actually involved in conceptual planning when completing Crack-the-Code. Successful, well-rounded performance on this task seems to require analyzing the task, generating hypotheses and testing them, and evaluating the entire process and attempting the task again if the result is not the required one. One child's performance seldom includes all of these components but the more components that are present, the better that performance will usually be.

DISCUSSION OF CONCEPTUAL PLANNING

Psychologists, like physicists, cannot free themselves from the effects of the instruments that they use—what we observe is invariably framed by the tests we choose to observe the phenomenon. In the studies discussed in this chapter, higher levels of planning were examined by using only the Planned Composition or the Crack-the-Code task. We have tried to identify the important parameters of these tasks as much as possible and to understand the nature of the mental activities that we have investigated through these tasks. More thorough protocol studies will be a welcome addition to this line of inquiry. It is important to know the parameters of the tasks as thoroughly as possible in order to understand the context of planning activities.

We certainly recommend the use of the Crack-the-Code task in future investigations on the lifespan development of planning. Its potential for unravelling the course of planning development during the school years, as well as the decline of the planning function in later life, is apparent. Its usefulness in determining managerial excellence is also evident. The presented studies provide a good case, to say the least, for using Crack-the-Code in future research in this area. The exciting possibilities provided by computer presentation of a task makes future research even more inviting. The computer version should provide information not only about accuracy and speed of solution but also about the strategies used by a subject since it records all of the moves that s/he has made. Information will also be available about the amount of time that a subject takes to consider moves and the amount of time that s/he actually takes to move the objects to their anticipated locations. This information may help us to differentiate between different styles of planning and to partially eliminate the use of verbal protocols, which are more laborious to analyze.

Planned composition of the type that we have discussed is a much more complex planning task and, like other planning tasks that approximate real-life situations, is more difficult to score objectively. Ratings are always subjective and the only way in which to increase their reliability is to increase the number of raters. Yet, even this may not produce a valid rating. A simple example involves the discrepancy between the ratings of essays of Delhi students made by a Canadian rater who is unfamiliar with the writing style of Delhi students and a professor from the students' institute in Delhi. Whereas the ratings would be more reliable if, say, five additional Canadian raters were used, they would all be distracted, in all likelihood, by the quaint writing style of the Delhi students and would therefore not give a rating that was the same, or as valid, as that of an Indian professor!

The subjective nature of rating was also a problem in Mishra's (1992) study on writing as it relates to planning. This study, however, did not have the cross-cultural complications described above—all subjects were Canadian students and the raters were Canadian graduate students and teachers. Mishra's subjects produced a narrative after looking at each of the pictures in the TOWL test. These narratives were then scored using the scales that we used in previous experiments for scoring Planned Composition. Only some raters seemed to have produced valid ratings, as evaluated by an external examiner, and therefore, only their ratings were used for establishing the positive relationship that Mishra found between lower level planning tests (such as Matching Numbers) and composition ratings.

Both Crack-the-Code and Planned Composition allow subjects to make flexible and free responses. In Crack-the-Code, the moves that an individual can make are not predetermined and s/he is free to choose between any of the colors presented (for example, red and blue) and various ways of proceeding. This freedom to respond is extensive in both the composition of narratives and in solving the strategic planning problems. The freedom to respond in several different ways is what makes these tasks measures of complex planning and, in terms of the three levels of planning presented in Chapter 2, measures of action as opposed to operation-planning. If the required response was completely predictable from task characteristics, planning would play no role in determining the subject's response. It cannot be argued, however, that these tasks represent activity-planning, since the plans that they call for are still responses to particular problem situations. Devising experimental tasks to assess activity-planning is inherently difficult, mainly because realizing one's life-goals typically takes years. This should not, however, prevent us from devising other indicators of activity-planning, such as biographical and structured interviews (see, for example, Nurmi, 1989), and relating them to more simple experimental measures. After all, good planning should be related to long-term decision making.

7

NEW DIRECTIONS

Everything has been thought of before; the difficulty is
in thinking of it again.

Goethe

In the 1960s a distinct shift took place within psychology, one
from a behavioristic to a cognitive view of mental events. The
change was heralded by many important publications but one
of the major landmarks was the new conceptualization of language
and language acquisition that emerged as the branch of psychology
we now call psycholinguistics and the publication in 1960 of
the book *Plans and the Structure of Behavior* (Miller et al.,
1960).

In Chapter 1, we described how the information-processing
approach literally overran the dominant behavioristic view. The
behaviorist goal was to describe and explain behavior without reference
to the mind. *Plans and the Structure of Behavior* placed cognitive
planning in a unique position at the center of human activity. Plans
can be well- or ill-structured but they lead the individual to a goal
state that s/he may change several times during the planning process.
Sometimes the goal may not be readily apparent, yet planning will
continue to occur as a nonconscious cognitive process.

In this final chapter we will choose one or two ideas from each of the first four chapters and suggest an empirical study that might be worthwhile to conduct. We begin with an idea discussed in Chapter 1, where we described planning as a stable individual characteristic. Specifically, some people are good planners, whereas others are poor planners in many situations. Yet during the course of the development of planning on a particular occasion, the process is unstable, perhaps as it should be. The interesting question, however, is: how does the individual set goals and respond to feedback while engaged in the planning process? Changing goals, making the planning process flexible, and ultimately arriving at a solution that an individual is likely to change after further review are sometimes done without conscious awareness. We might therefore ask: in an empirical study, under what conditions is the process of planning not entirely conscious? We know, for example, that when comparing a routine task with an innovative task that requires new plans, there will be large individual differences in the planning processes for the novel task. In Chapter 1, we found that the distinction between problem solving (even of a routine kind) and planning may lie in one important component: the anticipation of action. Anticipating or creating problems while securing a goal that is beneficial to the entire community thus becomes the central characteristic of a good planner. Also, a good planner, as was noted in Chapter 1, selects and manipulates his or her environment in order to create the most appropriate problems.

Would it not be exciting, then, to design a situation involving anticipatory planning that would be relevant to the community from which people were selected? One could then look out for specific criteria associated with being a good planner while these people were engaged in solving a culturally appropriate problem. One could, for example, have more than one observer or examiner recording whether or not (and to what extent) subjects anticipated future events and were thinking of a sequence of steps that were consistent with that anticipation and were also flexible. There would also be at least two distinct categories of planful behavior, routine and novel, that could be used when observing these individuals. While many subjects could execute the programs once these were clearly given or left in front of them, only a few subjects would exhibit anticipatory programming, flexible use of information, and consistent changes in their plans as they approached a goal.

In Chapter 2, we presented a model of planning that included three levels of analysis: activity, action, and operation. This conceptualization of planning is based on the theory of activity first suggested by Vygotsky and then modified and developed further by Leontjev. The three-level model of planning has intuitive value in attempting to integrate within one framework diverse findings in the planning literature. What we still need, however, are empirical studies that would include measures of all three levels of planning and then explore the interrelationships between them. We all know of someone or the other who appears to be a bright and capable problem solver but time after time ends up making wrong choices in his or her life. Thus, it seems that problem solving (operation or action-planning) does not always correlate with activity planning. A factor analytic study, for example, including both operation-planning measures (such as Visual Search and easy items of Matching Numbers presented in Chapter 5), and action-planning measures (such as Crack-the-Code and Planned Composition described in Chapter 6, or different kinds of errand scheduling tasks reviewed in Chapter 4), as well as activity-planning measures, would certainly help us to understand better how the three levels of planning are related.

Activity-planning, the highest level in our model, is the most difficult to study. One possibility would be to conduct structured interviews with the participants about their future plans and how they intend to realize these plans. Nurmi (1989), for example, used this approach and then coded his participants' (11- and 15-year-old adolescents) responses according to the level of planning they indicated. But, for the most part, developing appropriate measures for activity-planning remains a challenge for future research.

In Chapter 2, we also discussed planning within the context of a reexamination of intelligence, which we conceptualized as consisting of four major processes, with planning perhaps being the highest of the four processes in the hierarchy. We wish to emphasize here that a person can plan well or poorly depending on the knowledge base that s/he has acquired, and his or her use of the three other major processes (i.e., attention, simultaneous processing, and successive processing). To the extent that any of these cognitive components are deficient, however, planning will be deficient. A worthwhile experiment might involve controlling the influx of information into the knowledge base and observing how the course of planning is altered.

In Chapter 3 we discussed planning from a neuropsychological perspective. Although our knowledge of the anatomy and physiology of the frontal lobes, as they relate to the cognitive processes of planning and decision making, is still very limited, we now know much about testing the various possible functions or dysfunctions associated with frontal lobe injury. In India, literally thousands of people experience minor accidents when they fall off a two-wheeled vehicle (especially motor scooters) or rickshaws. The possible dysfunctions that such apparently innocuous falls may produce represent an excellent area for possible study. Such research would be valuable not only for understanding the relationship between planning functions and closed head injuries but more importantly, for advising the injured individual and his or her family members about the consequences of the injury and for guiding them through the rehabilitation process. In Chapters 5 and 6, we have already presented several tests that would be quite suitable for monitoring planning dysfunctions and we know the parameters of these tests as given in ·those chapters. It would indeed be a useful project to test and map out the injured individual's cognitive functions, including the four major processes—i.e., PASS—and to then determine if and in what manner these functions, as expressed in planning and decision making, appear to have been damaged.·

Continuing with the research opportunities with individuals who exhibit neuropsychological dysfunctions, specifically in the frontal lobes, a fertile line of investigation concerns the effects of early versus late damage. It is now generally accepted that early damage to frontal lobes has a much more debilitating effect than later damage. This is the reverse of what happens in regard to posterior part of the brain—the earlier damage can be compensated for by other intact areas of the brain. Why is the frontal damage in early years so disastrous for cognitive as well as social functions? The reason is believed to be the critical role played by the frontal lobes "in the synaptic selection process by periodically reorganizing the synaptic environment of posterior cortical regions" (Thatcher, 1992, p. 591). Frontal lobes play a crucial part in the 'pruning' process of excess synapses that are produced at different stages of development of the brain starting from prenatal stage to age 16. The plasticity of the brain thus consists of genetically programmed overproduction of synapses and the environmentally determined maintenance and pruning of synaptic connections (Thatcher, 1992).

Depending on the time and location of frontal cortical injury, the long-term behavioral consequences should vary, and in any case, they should be markedly different from the consequences of more posterior lesions. Thus, a long-term study correlating the time and location of brain injuries to their behavioral consequences as well as to the effects of remediation in different phases would be most beneficial in advancing our understanding of this complex organ and its significance for cognitive development.

In Chapter 4, the development of planning was discussed. The development of planning as it is modified by the context, both cultural and physical, within which the child develops, has not been examined systematically. There are a number of ways in which such studies could be designed, one of which could involve the effects of schooling. In many parts of India, there still exist school-aged children who do not attend school. Thus, the question is not only how planning develops in these unschooled children as compared to schooled children but how, generally, the cultural aspects of planning are transmitted. Specifically, does cultural transmission occur through spontaneous and informal education or largely through schooling? What kinds of cultural decision-making skills are specifically related to schooling? Provided that all other conditions remain the same, schooled and unschooled children can thus be examined in relation to the development of planning.

Another area of study that has not been prominent enough as yet is the description of change processes. The two questions frequently asked by researchers studying cognitive development are: (a) what is changing or developing, and (b) how that change is accomplished (see, for example, Siegler, 1994; Thelen, 1992). However, these questions have not been answered adequately and most accounts or theories of development have emphasized "identifying sequences of one-to-one correspondences between ages and ways of thinking or acting, rather than specifying how these changes occur" (Siegler, 1994, p. 1).

This is partly due to methodological shortcomings. Current methods of inquiry tend to conceal rather than to capture possible mechanisms of change, such as intra-individual variability and the effect of practice, for example. Fischer and Silvern (1985, p. 643) suggest that we need assessment techniques that "allow the detection of individual differences in developmental sequences" and are "sensitive to the possibility that people reason differently, not just more or less maturely".

While identifying general trends and one-to-one correspondence may be essential for designing age-appropriate teaching methods and curriculum, a more detailed study of the mechanisms and sources of variation in development may be necessary for designing successful interventions in special education, especially in the burgeoning field of cognitive remediation. Variability, for example, appears to play a critical role in learning (Siegler, 1994). Siegler suggests that within-subject variability is largest in trials immediately before a discovery and during the trial in which the discovery is made. Accordingly, large within-subject variability should be useful for identifying a student's zone of proximal development (Vygotsky, 1978) within which an intervention should benefit the student most. But variability also implies that what is good for one child is not necessarily good for another. Thus, identifying between-subjects variability in their preferred mode of processing information, for example, is as essential for successful interventions as is within subject variability.

The question remains: how do we identify both general trends and individual differences in development? Using verbal protocols or other suitable process data from studies including several measures of action-planning tasks should give us that information about the development of planning. One such study was briefly described in Chapter 6, but a similar design could be easily adjusted to include more tasks and other process measures that may be more suitable for experimental purposes. Moreover, designs including several items of same difficulty would be beneficial in verifying the significance of variablity and practice in learning.

In Chapters 5 and 6 we discussed several concrete studies of planning, some of which leave various questions unanswered. It is the task of researchers to use these experiments as stepping stones for producing research that is socially valuable and culturally appropriate.

We hope that this monograph will be used as an information source for the theoretical work that we have presented and for the empirical studies that this work has generated. Planning is a characteristic unique to human beings; it is an important aspect of cultural learning and can be observed as easily within the constraints of the laboratory as in behavior in the outside world. It is our hope that the knowledge contained in this monograph can be used to generate imaginative and culturally relevant research.

REFERENCES

Allport, D. A. (1980). Attention and performance. In G. Claxton (Ed.), *Cognitive psychology* (pp. 112-153). London: Routledge & Kegan Paul.

Anderson, J. R. (1993). Problem solving and learning. *American Psychologist, 48*, 35-44.

Ashman, A. F. (1978). *The relationship between planning and simultaneous and successive synthesis.* Unpublished doctoral dissertation, University of Alberta, Edmonton, Canada.

Ashman, A. F., & Conway, R. N. F. (1989). *Cognitive strategies for special education.* New York: Routledge.

Ashman, A. F., & Das, J. P. (1980). Relation between planning and simultaneous-successive processing. *Perceptual and Motor Skills, 51*, 371-382.

Atkinson, R., & Shiffrin, R. (1968). Human memory: A proposed system and its control processes. In K.W. Spence, & J.T. Spence (Eds.), *The psychology of learning and motivation: Advances in theory and research.* New York: Academic Press.

Baker-Sennett, J., Matusov, E., & Rogoff, B. (1993). Planning as developmental process. In H. W. Reese (Ed.), *Advances in child development and behavior* (pp. 253-281). San Diego: Academic Press.

Bartlett, F. C. (1932). *Remembering, a study in experimental and social psychology.* New York: Macmillan.

————. (1958). *Thinking: An experimental and social study.* London: Allen & Unwin.

Becker, M. G., Isaac, W., & Hynd, G. W. (1987). Neuropsychological development of nonverbal behaviors attributed to "frontal lobe" functioning. *Developmental Neuropsychology, 3*, 275-298.

Belmont, J. M., & Mitchell, D. W. (1987). The general strategies hypothesis as applied to cognitive theory in mental retardation. *Intelligence, 11*, 91-105.

Black, I. B. (1991). *Information in the brain: A molecular perspective.* Cambridge, MA: The MIT Press.

Bridgeman, B. (1993). The Computational Brain by P. S. Churland and T. J. Sejnowski [13 paragraphs]. *Psyche,* [On-line serial] *7*(1). Available FTP: 130.194.64.2 Directory: psyche.

Broadbent, D. E. (1958). *Perception and communication.* New York: Pergamon Press.

Broadbent, D., Fitzgerald, P., & Broadbent, M. (1986). Implicit and explicit knowledge in the control of complex systems. *British Journal of Psychology, 77,* 33-50.

Brown, A. L., & Campione, J. C. (1986). Academic intelligence and learning potential. In R. J. Sternberg, & D. K. Detterman (Eds.), *What is intelligence? Contemporary viewpoints on its nature and definition.* New York: Ablex.

Brown, A. L., & Deloache, J. S. (1978). Skills, plans and self-regulation. In R. S. Siegler (Ed.), *Children's thinking: What develops?* Hillsdale, NJ: Erlbaum.

Brown, A. L., Bransford, J. D., Ferrara, R. A., & Campione, J. C. (1983). Learning, remembering and understanding. In P. H. Mussen (Ed.), *Handbook of child psychology* (4th ed.) (Vol. 3, pp. 77-166). New York: Wiley.

Bruner, J. S., Goodnow, J., & Austin, G. (1956). *A study of thinking.* New York: Wiley.

Carlson, J. S., & Wiedl, K. H. (1988). The dynamic assessment of intelligence. In H. C. Haywood, & D. Tzuriel (Eds.), *Interactive Assessment.* Potomoc, MD: Erlbaum.

Carroll, J. B. (1953). *The study of language.* Cambridge, MA: Harvard University Press.

―――― (1964). *Language and thought.* Englewood Cliffs, NJ: Prentice-Hall.

Case, R. (1985). *Intellectual development: Birth to adulthood.* New York: Academic.

Chomsky, N. (1957). *Syntactic structures.* The Hague: Mouton.

Clancey, W. J. (1991). Review of Rosenfield's "The Invention of Memory". *Artificial Intelligence, 50* (2), 241-284.

Cohen, J., Dunbar, K., & McClelland, J. (1990). On the control of automatic processes: A parallel distributed processing account of the Stroop effect. *Psychological Review, 97,* 332-361.

Damasio, A. R. (1985). The frontal lobes. In K. Heilman, & E. Valenstein (Eds.), *Clinical neuropsychology* (2nd ed., pp. 339-375). New York: Oxford University Press.

Das, J. P. (1973). Structure of cognitive abilities: Evidence for simultaneous and successive processing. *Journal of Educational Psychology, 65,* 103-108.

―――― (1980). Planning: Theoretical considerations and empirical evidence. *Psychological Report, 41,* 141-151.

―――― (1984a). Aspects of planning. In J. R. Kirby (Ed.), *Cognitive strategies and educational performance* (pp. 35-50). New York: Academic Press.

―――― (1984b). Intelligence and information integration. In J. R. Kirby (Ed.), *Cognitive strategies and educational performance* (pp. 13-31). New York: Academic Press.

―――― (1988). Simultaneous-Successive Processing and Planning. In R. Schmeck (Ed.), *Learning Styles & Learning Strategies* (pp. 101-129). New York: Plenum.

―――― (1989). A system for cognitive assessment and its advantage over IQ. In D. Vickers, & P. L. Smith (Eds.), *Human information processing: Measures, mechanisms, and models* (pp. 535-546). North-Holland: Elsevier.

Das, J. P. (1994). Eastern views of intelligence. In R. J. Sternberg (ed.), *Encyclopedia of Intelligence*. New York: Macmillan.

Das, J. P., & **Dash, U. N.** (1990). Schooling, literacy and cognitive development: A study in rural India. In C. K. Leong & B. S. Randhawa (Eds.), *Understanding literacy and cognition: Theory, research and application* (pp. 217-244). New York: Plenum Press.

Das, J. P., & **Heemsbergen, D. B.** (1983). Planning as a factor in the assessment of cognitive processes. *Journal of Psychoeducational Assessment, 1,* 1-15.

Das, J. P., Kirby, J. R., & **Jarman, R. F.** (1975). Simultaneous and successive synthesis: An alternative model. *Psychological Bulletin, 82,* 87-103.

———— (1979). *Simultaneous and successive cognitive processes.* New York: Academic.

Das, J. P., Misra, S., & **Mishra, R. K.** (1993). Assessing ability for strategic planning. *Vikalpa, 18* (3), 29-36.

Das, J. P., & **Naglieri, J. A.** (1993). *Das–Naglieri Cognitive Assessment System* (standardization version). Chicago: Riverside Publishing Company.

Das, J. P., Naglieri, J. A., & **Kirby, J. R.** (1994). *Assessment of cognitive processes.* Needham Heights, MA: Allyn and Bacon.

De Bono, E. (1986). *The uses of lateral thinking.* London: Penguin Books.

De Lisi, R. (1987). A cognitive-developmental model of planning. In S. L. Friedman, E. K. Scholnick, & R. R. Cocking (Eds.), *Blueprints for thinking* (pp. 79-109). New York: Cambridge University Press.

DeLoache, J. S., & **Brown, A. L.** (1987). The early emergence of planning skills in children. In J. Bruner & H. Haste (Eds.), *Making sense* (pp. 108-130). New York: Methuen.

Denckla, M. B., & **Rudel, R.** (1976). Naming of object drawings by dyslexic and other learning disabled children. *Brain and Language, 3,* 1-15.

Diamond, A. (1985). The development of the ability to use recall to guide action, as indicated by infants' performance on AB. *Child Development, 56,* 868-883.

————, (1991). Frontal lobe involvement in cognitive changes during the first year of life. In K. R. Gibson, & A. N. Petersen (Eds.), *Brain maturation and cognitive development* (pp. 127-180). New York: Aldine de Gruyter.

Diamond, A., & **Goldman-Rakic, P. S.** (1983). Comparison of performance on a Piagetian object permanence task in human infants and rhesus monkeys: Evidence for involvement of prefrontal cortex. *Neuroscience Abstracts, 9,* 641.

————, (1985). Evidence for involvement of prefrontal cortex in cognitive changes during the first year of life: Comparison of human infants and rhesus monkeys on a detour task with transparent barrier. *Neuroscience Abstracts, 11,* 832.

————, (1986). Comparative development in human infants and infant rhesus monkeys of cognitive functions that depend on prefrontal cortex. *Neuroscience Abstracts, 12,* 742.

————, (1989). Comparison of human infants and rhes monkeys on Piaget's AB task: Evidence for dependence on dorsolateral prefrontal cortex. *Experimental Brain Research, 74,* 24-40.

Diamond, A., Zola-Morgan, S., & **Squire, L.** (1989). Successful performance by monkeys with lesions of the hippocampal formation on AB and Object Retrieval, two tasks that mark developmental changes in human infants. *Behavioral Neuroscience, 103,* 526-537.

Diaz, R. M., Neal, C. J., & **Amaya-Williams, M.** (1990). The social origins of self-regulation. In L. C. Moll (Ed.), *Vygotsky and education* (pp. 127-154). New York: Cambridge University Press.

Dimant, R. J., & **Bearison, D. J.** (1991). Development of formal reasoning during successive peer interactions. *Development Psychology, 27*, 277-284.

Donald, M. (1993). Précis of Origins of the modern mind: Three stages in the evolution of culture and cognition. *Behavioral and Brain Sciences, 16*, 737-791.

Dreher, M., & **Oerter, R.** (1987). Action planning competencies during adolescence and early adulthood. In S. L. Friedman, E. K. Scholnick, & R. R. Cocking (Eds.), *Blueprints for thinking* (pp. 321-355). New York: Cambridge University Press.

Duncan, J., & **Humphreys, G. W.** (1989). Visual search and stimulus similarity. *Psychological Review, 96*, 433-458.

Eaking, S. E., & **Douglas, V.** (1971). "Automatization" and oral reading problems in children. *Journal of Learning Disabilities, 4*, 31-38.

Egeth, H., Jonides, J., & **Wall, S.** (1972). Parallel processing of multi-element displays. *Cognitive Psychology, 3*, 674-698.

Eglin, M., Robertson, L. C., & **Knight, R. T.** (1991). Cortical substrates supporting visual search in humans. *Cerebral Cortex, 1*, 262-272.

Epstein, W., & **Broota, K. D.** (1986). Automatic and attentional components in perception of size-at-a-distance. *Perception and psychophysics, 4*, 256-269.

Epstein, W., & **Lovitts, B. E.** (1985). Automatic and attentional components in perception of shape-at-a-slant. *Journal of Experimental Psychology: Human Perception & Performance, 11*, 355-366.

Ericsson, K. A., & **Simon, H. A.** (1980). Verbal reports as data. *Psychological Review, 87*, 215-251.

———— (1993). *Protocol analysis: Verbal reports as data.* (Rev. Ed.). Cambridge, MA: The MIT Press.

Estes, W. (1982). Learning, memory, and intelligence. In R. Sternberg (Ed.), *Handbook of human intelligence* (pp. 170-224). Cambridge, MA: Cambridge University Press.

Eysenck, M. W. (1984). *A handbook of cognitive psychology.* Hillsdale, NJ: Lawrence Erlbaum.

Feuerstein, R. (1979). *The dynamic assessment of retarded performers: The learning potential assessment device, theory, instruments, and techniques.* Baltimore: University Park Press.

Fischer, K. W. & **Silvern, L.** (1985). Stages and individual differences in cognitive development. *Annual Review of Psychology, 36*, 613-648.

Fisk, A. D., & **Schneider, W.** (1983). Category and word search: Generalizing search principles to complex processing. *Journal of Experimental Psychology: Learning, Memory and Cognition, 9*, 177-194.

Friedman, S. L., Scholnick, E. K., & **Cocking, R. R.** (1987). Reflections on reflections: What planning is and how it develops. In S. L. Friedman, E. K. Scholnick, & R. R. Cocking (Eds.), *Blueprints for thinking* (pp. 515-534). New York: Cambridge University Press.

Fuster, J. M. (1989). *The prefrontal cortex* (2nd ed.). New York: Raven Press.

Gardner, W., & **Rogoff, B.** (1990). Children's deliberateness of planning according to task circumstances. *Developmental Psychology, 26*, 480-487.

Garner, W. R. (1962). *Uncertainty and structure as psychological concepts.* New York: Wiley.

Gauvain, M., & Rogoff, B. (1989). Collaborative problem solving and children's planning skills. *Developmental Psychology, 25,* 139-151.

_____ (1989). Collaborative problem solving and children's planning skills. *Developmental Psychology, 25,* 139-151.

Glass, A. L., & Holyoak, K. J. (1986). *Cognition* (2nd ed.). New York: Random House.

Goldberg, E., & Bilder, R. M. Jr. (1987). The frontal lobes and hierarchical organization of cognitive control. In E. Perecman (Ed.), *The frontal lobes revisited* (pp. 159-187). New York: IRBN Press.

Golden, C. J. (1981). The Luria-Nebraska children's battery: Theory and formulation. In G. W. Hynd, & J. E. Orbzut (Eds.), *Neuropsychological assessment and the school-age child* (pp. 277-302). London: Grune & Stratton.

Goldman-Rakic, P. S. (1992). Working memory and the mind. *Scientific American, 267* (3), 111-117.

Goodnow, J. J. (1987). Social aspects of planning. In S. L. Friedman, E. K. Scholnick, & R. R. Cocking (Eds.), *Blueprints for thinking* (pp. 179-201). New York: Cambridge University Press.

Grabowecky, M., Robertson, L. C., & Treisman, A. (1993). Preattentive processes guide visual search: Evidence from patients with unilateral visual neglect. *Journal of Cognitive Neuroscience, 5,* 288-302.

Greenfield, P. M. (1991). Language, tools and brain: The ontogeny and phylogeny of hierarchically organized sequential behavior. *Behavioral and Brain Sciences, 14,* 531-595.

Greeno, J., Riley, M. S., & Gelman, R. (1984). Conceptual competence and children's counting. *Cognitive Psychology, 16,* 94-143.

Guthrie, E. R. (1935). *The psychology of learning.* New York: Harper.

Hammill, D. D., & Larsen, S. C. (1988). *Test of written language-2.* Austin, TX: Pro-Ed.

Hasher, L., & Zacks, R. T. (1979). Automatic and effortful processes in memory. *Journal of Experimental Psychology: General, 108,* 356-388.

Hayes-Roth, B., & Hayes-Roth, F. (1979). A cognitive model of planning. *Cognitive Science, 3,* 275-310.

Hebb, D. O. (1960). The American Revolution. *American Psychologist, 15,* 735-745.

Hecaen, H., & Albert, M. (1978). *Human neuropsychology.* New York: John Wiley & Sons.

Hilgard, E. R., & Bower, G. H. (1966). *Theories of learning* (3rd. ed.). New York: Appleton-Century-Crofts.

Hudspeth, W. J., & Pribram, K. H. (1990). Stages of brain and cognitive maturation. *Journal of Educational Psychology, 82,* 881-884.

Hynd, G. W., & Willis, W. G. (1988). *Pediatric neuropsychology.* London: Grune & Stratton.

James, W. (1904). *The principles of psychology.* New York: Holt.

_____ (1958). *The varieties of religious experience.* New York: New American Library.

Jarman, R. F., Vavrik, J., & Walton, P. D. (1995). Metacognitive and frontal lobe processes: At the interface of cognitive psychology and neuropsychology. *Genetic psychology monographs.*

Jensen, A. R. (1987). Individual differences in hick paradigm. In P. A. Vernon (Ed.), *Speed of information-processing and intelligence* (pp. 101-175). Norwood, NJ: Ablex.

Jonides, J., & Gleitman, H. A. (1972). Conceptual category effect in visual search: 0 as letter or as digit. *Perception and Psychophysics, 12,* 457-460.

Kahneman, D., & Henik, A. (1981). Perceptual organization and. attention. In M. Kubovy, & J. R. Pomerantz (Eds.), *Perceptual organization.* Hillsdale, NJ: Erlbaum.

Kahneman, D., Treisman, A., & Burkell, J. (1983). The cost of visual filtering. *Journal of Experimental Psychology: Human perception and performance, 9,* 510-522.

Kandel, E. R., & Schwartz, J. H. (1985). *Principles of neural science* (2nd ed.). New York: Elsevier.

Kar, B. C. (1989). *Studies and planning as a cognitive process: Theoretical and operational considerations.* Unpublished doctoral dissertation, Utkal University, Bhubaneswar, India.

Kar, B. C., & Dash, U. N. (1988). Development of visual search as a function of mapping condition, field density and field stimuli. *Indian Psychologist, 5,* 41-50.

———— (1992). The information integration model: A strategy to study cognitive growth. In A. K. Srivastava (Ed.), *Researches in child and adolescent psychology.* New Delhi: NCERT Publications.

Kar, B. C., Dash, U. N., Das, J. P., & Carlson, J. (1993). Two experiments on the dynamic assessment of planning. *Learning and Individual Differences, 5,* 13-29.

Kar, B. C., & Nanda, J. (1993). *Dynamic assessment of coding and planning in schooled and unschooled children.* Unpublished research, Department of Psychology, Utkal University, Bhubaneswar, India.

Kearins, J. M. (1981). Visual spatial memory in Australian aboriginal children of desert regions. *Cognitive Psychology, 13,* 434-460.

———— (1986). Visual spatial memory in aboriginal and white Australian children. *Australian Journal of Psychology, 38,* 203-214.

Kirby, J. (1984). Educational role of cognitive plans and strategies. In J. Kirby (Ed.), *Cognitive strategies and educational performance* (pp. 51-88). Orlando: Academic Press.

Kirby, J. R., & Moore, P. (1987). Metacognitive awareness about reading and its relation to reading ability. *Journal of Psychoeducational Assessment, 2,* 119-137.

Kitchener, K. S. (1983). Cognition, metacognition, and epistemic cognition: A three-level model of cognitive processing. *Human Development, 26,* 222-232.

Klahr, D., & Robinson, M. (1981). Formal assessment of problem-solving and planning processes in preschool children. *Cognitive Psychology, 13,* 113-148.

Köhler, W. (1959/1927). *The mentality of apes.* New York: Vintage Books.

Kontos, S. (1983). Adult-child interaction and the origins of metacognition. *Journal of Educational Research, 77,* 43-54.

Korf, R. E. (1987). Planning as search: A quantitative approach. *Artificial Intelligence, 33,* 65-88.

Kozulin, A. (1986a). The concept of activity in Soviet psychology: Vygotsky, his disciples and critics. *American Psychologist, 41,* 264-274.

────── (1986b). Introduction. In L. S. Vygotsky, *Thought and language.* Cambridge, MA: The MIT Press.

Kreitler, S., & Kreitler, H. (1987). Conceptions and processes of planning: The developmental perspective. In S. L. Friedman, E. K. Scholnick, & R. R. Cocking (Eds.), *Blueprints for thinking* (pp. 205-272). New York: Cambridge University Press.

Kristofferson, M. W. (1972). Effects of practice on character classification performance. *Canadian Journal of Psychology, 26,* 54-60.

LaBerge, D., & Samuels, S. J. (1974). Toward a theory of automatic information processing in reading. *Cognitive Psychology, 6,* 293-323.

Lachman, R., Lachman, J. L., & Butterfield, E. C. (1979). *Cognitive psychology and information processing: An introduction.* Hillsdale, NJ: Erlbaum.

Lawson, M. (1980). Metamemory: Making decisions about strategies. In J. Kirby, & J. Biggs (Eds.), *Cognition, development and instruction* (pp. 145-160). New York: Academic Press.

────── (1984). Being executive about metacognition. In J. Kirby (Ed.), *Cognitive strategies and educational performance* (pp. 89-110). Orlando, FL: Academic Press.

Lawson, M. J., & Rice, D. N. (1987). Thinking aloud: Analysing students' mathematics performance. *School Psychology International, 8,* 233-243.

Lee, B. (1987). Recontextualizing Vygotsky. In M. Hickmann (Ed.), *Social and functional approaches to language and thought* (pp. 87-104). New York: Academic Press.

Leontjev, A. N. (1978). *Activity, consciousness, and personality.* Englewood Cliffs, NJ: Prentice-Hall.

────── (1979). The problem of activity in psychology. In J. V. Wertsch (Ed.), *The concept of activity in Soviet psychology* (pp. 37-71). New York: M. E. Sharpe.

Levin, H. S., Culhane, K. A., Hartmann, J., Evankovich, K., Mattson, A. J., Harward, H., Ringholz, G., Ewing-Cobbs, L., & Fletcher, J. M. (1991). Developmental changes in performance on tests of purported frontal lobe functioning. *Developmental Neuropsychology, 6,* 377-395.

Levina, R. E. (1979). L. S. Vygotsky's ideas about the planning function of speech in children. In J. V. Wertsch (Ed.), *The concept of activity in Soviet psychology,* (pp. 279-299). New York: M. E. Sharpe.

Lezak, M. D. (1983). *Neuropsychological assessment.* (2nd. ed.). New York: Oxford University Press.

Logan, G. D. (1978). Attention in character classification: Evidence for the automaticity of component stages. *Journal of Experimental Psychology: General, 107,* 32-63.

────── (1979). On the use of a concurrent memory load to measure attention and automaticity. *Journal of Experimental Psychology: Human Perception and Performance, 5,* 189-207.

────── (1980). Attention and automaticity in Stroop and priming tasks: Theory and data. *Cognitive Psychology, 12,* 523-553.

────── (1988). Toward an instance theory of automatization. *Psychological Review, 95,* 492-527.

Logan, G. D., & Klapp, S. T. (1991). Automatizing alphabet arithmetic: I. Is extended practice necessary to produce automaticity? *Journal of Experimental Psychology: Learning, Memory, and Cognition, 17,* 179-195.

Luria, A. R. (1959). The directive function of speech in development and dissolution. *Word, 15,* 341-352.

———— (1966). *Human brain and psychological processes.* New York: Harper & Row.

———— (1970). *Traumatic aphasia.* The Hague: Mouton.

———— (1973a). *The working brain.* New York: Basic Books.

———— (1973b). The origin and cerebral organization of man's conscious action. In S. G. Sapir, & A. C. Nitzburg (Eds.), *Children with learning problems* (pp. 109-130). New York: Brunner/Mazel.

———— (1976). *Cognitive development: Its cultural and social foundations.* Cambridge, MA: Harvard University Press.

———— (1980). *Higher cortical functions in man* (2nd. ed.). New York: Basic Books.

———— (1982). *Language and cognition.* New York: John Wiley & Sons.

Luria, A. R., & **Tsvetkova, L. S.** (1990). *The neuropsychological analysis of problem solving.* Orlando, FL: Paul M. Deutsch Press.

Luria, A. R., & **Yudovich, F. I.** (1959). *Speech and the development of mental processes in the child.* London: Staples Press.

Marcel, A. J. (1983). Conscious and unconscious perception: An approach to the relations between phenomenal experience and perceptual processes. *Cognitive Psychology, 15,* 238-300.

Mathur, P., & **Das, J. P.** (1994). Manuscript in preparation.

McCarthy, R. A., & **Warrington, E. K.** (1990). *Cognitive neuropsychology.* London: Academic Press.

McNeill, D. (1987). *Psycholinguistics: A new approach.* New York: Harper & Row.

Miller, G. A., Galanter, E. H., & **Pribram, K. H.** (1960). *Plans and the structure of behavior.* New York: Holt, Rinehart & Winston.

Mishra, R. K. (1992). *Planning in writing: Evidence from cognitive tests and think-aloud protocols.* Unpublished doctoral dissertation, University of Alberta, Edmonton, Canada.

Mohapatra, M. (1990). *Developmental changes in controlled search.* Unpublished M.Phil. thesis, Utkal University, Bhubaneswar, India.

Naglieri, J. A. (1989). A cognitive processing theory for the measurement of intelligence. *Educational Psychologist, 24*(2), 185-206.

Naglieri, J. A., & **Das, J. P.** (1987). Construct and criterion-related validity of planning, simultaneous, and successive cognitive processing tasks. *Journal of Psychoeducational Assessment, 4,* 353-363.

———— (1988). Planning-Arousal-Simultaneous-Successive (PASS): A model for assessment. *Journal of School Psychology, 26,* 35-48.

———— (1990). Planning, attention, simultaneous and successive (PASS) cognitive processes as a model for intelligence. *Journal of Psychoeducational Assessment, 8,* 303-337.

Naglieri, J. A., Das, J. P., Stevens, J. J., & **Ledbetter, M. F.** (1991). Confirmatory factor analysis of planning, attention, simultaneous, and successive cognitive processing tasks. *Journal of School Psychology, 29,* 1-17.

Naglieri, J. A., Prewett, P. N., & **Bardos, A. N.** (1989). An exploratory study of planning, attention, simultaneous, and successive cognitive processes. *Journal of School Psychology, 27,* 347-364.

Nanda, J. (1990). *Boundary conditions in visual search and target-location relationship.* Unpublished M.A. thesis, Utkal University, Bhubaneswar, India.

Navon, D. (1984). Resources—A theoretical soup stone? *Psychological Review, 91*, 216-234.

Navon, D., & Gopher, D. (1979). On the economy of the human processing system. *Psychological Review, 86*, 214-255.

Neisser, U. (1967). *Cognitive psychology.* New York: Appleton Century Crofts.

Newcomer, P. L., & Barenbaum, E. M. (1991). The written composition ability of children with learning disabilities: A review of literature from 1980 to 1990. *Journal of Learning Disabilities, 24*, 578-593.

Newell, A., & Simon, H. A. (1972). *Human problem solving.* Englewood Cliffs, NJ: Prentice-Hall.

Newell, A., Shaw, J. C., & Simon, H. A. (1958a). Chess-playing problems and the problem of complexity. *IBM Journal of Research and Development, 2*, 320-335.

———— (1958b). Elements of a theory of human problem solving. *Psychological Review, 65*, 151-166.

———— (1959). Report on general problem-solving program. Proceedings of the International Conference on Information Processing, Paris.

Nurmi, J. (1989). Development of orientation to the future during early adolescence: A four-year longitudinal study and two cross-sectional comparisons. *International Journal of Psychology, 2*, 195-214.

Oppenheimer, L. (1987). Cognitive and social variables in the plan of action. In S. L. Friedman, E. K. Scholnick, & R. R. Cocking (Eds.), *Blueprints for thinking* (pp. 356-392). New York: Cambridge University Press.

Ornstein, R. E. (1972). *The psychology of consciousness.* San Francisco: W. H. Freeman and Company.

Paris, S., Newman, R., & McVey, K. (1982). Learning the functional significance and mnemonic actions: A microgenetic study of strategy acquisition. *Journal of Experimental Child Psychology, 34*, 490-509.

Parrila, R. K. (1995). Vygotskian views on language and planning in children. *School Psychology International, 16*, 167-183.

Parrila, R. K., & Papadopoulos, T. C. (1994). *Developmental Aspects of Planning.* Paper presented at the CSSE conference in Calgary, Canada.

Parrila, R. K., Äystö, S., & Das, J. P. (1994). Development of planning in relation to age, attention, simultaneous, and successive processing. *Journal of Psychoeducational Assessment, 12*, 212-227.

Parrill-Burnstein, M. (1978). Teaching kindergarten children to solve problems: An information-processing approach. *Child Development, 49*, 700-706.

Passler, M. A., Isaac, W., & Hynd, G. W. (1985). Neuropsychological development of behaviors attributed to frontal lobe functioning in children. *Developmental Neuropsychology, 1*, 349-370.

Pattnaik, B. (1992). *Boundary conditions in word search: Developmental changes.* Unpublished M.A. thesis, Utkal University, Bhubaneswar, India.

Pavlov, I. P. (1928). *Lectures on conditioned reflex (Vol. 1).* New York: International Publishers.

———— (1942). *Lectures on conditioned reflex (Vol. 2).* New York: International Publishers.

Pea, R. D. (1982). What is planning development the development of? In D. Forbes, & M. T. Greenberg (Eds.), *New directions for child development: Children's planning strategies* (Vol. 18, pp. 5-26). San Francisco: Jossey-Bass.

Pea, R. D., & Hawkins, J. (1987). Planning in the chore-scheduling task. In S. L. Friedman, E. K. Scholnick, & R. R. Cocking (Eds.), *Blueprints for thinking* (pp. 273-302). New York: Cambridge University Press.

Perecman, E. (1987). Consciousness and the meta-functions of the frontal lobes: Setting the Stage. In E. Perecman (Ed.), *The frontal lobes revisited* (pp. 1-10). New York: IRBN Press.

Piaget, J. (1963). *The origins of intelligence in children.* New York: Norton.

———— (1976). *The grasp of consciousness.* Cambridge, MA: Harvard University Press.

Posner, M. I. (1978). *Chronometric explorations of mind.* Hillsdale, NJ: Erlbaum.

Posner, M. I., & Petersen, S. E. (1990). The attention system of the human brain. *Annual Review of Neuroscience, 13,* 25-42.

Posner, M. I., & Snyder, C. R. R. (1975). Attention and cognitive control. In R. L. Solso (Ed.), *Information processing and cognition* (pp. 55-85). Hillsdale, NJ: Erlbaum.

Pribram, K. H. (1973). The primate frontal cortex—Executive of the brain. In K. H. Pribram, & A. R. Luria (Eds.), *Psychophysiology of the frontal lobes* (pp. 293-314). New York: Academic.

Radziszewska, B., & Rogoff, B. (1988). Influence of adult and peer collaborators on children's planning skills. *Developmental Psychology, 24,* 840-848.

———— (1991). Children's guided participation in planning imaginary errands with skilled adult or peer partners. *Developmental Psychology, 27,* 381-389.

Rogoff, B. (1981). Schooling and the development of cognitive skills. In H. C. Triandis, & A. Heron (Eds), *Handbook of cross-cultural psychology* (Vol. 4). Boston: Allyn & Bacon.

———— (1991). Social interaction as apprenticeship in thinking: Guidance and participation in spatial planning. In L. B. Resnick, J. L. Levine, & S. D. Teasley (Eds.), *Perspectives on socially shared cognition* (pp. 349-364). Washington, DC: APA.

Rogoff, B., Gauvain, M., & Gardner, W. (1987). The development of children's skills in adjusting plans to circumstances. In S. L. Friedman, E. K. Scholnick, & R. R. Cocking (Eds.), *Blueprints for thinking* (pp. 303-320). New York: Cambridge University Press.

Rommetveit, R. (1979). On the architecture of intersubjectivity. In R. Rommetveit & R. M. Blakar (Eds.), *Studies of language, thought and verbal communication* (pp. 93-107). New York: Academic Press.

Sacerdoti, E. D. (1977). *A structure for plans and behavior.* Amsterdam: Elsevier.

Schank, R. C., & Abelson, R. P. (1977). *Scripts, plans, goals, and understanding.* Hillsdale, NJ: Erlbaum.

Schneider, W., & Shiffrin, R. M. (1977). Controlled and automatic human information processing: I. Detection, search, and attention. *Psychological Review, 84,* 1-66.

Scholnick, E. K., & Friedman, S. L. (1987). The planning construct in the psychological literature. In S. L. Friedman, E. K. Scholnick, & R. R. Cocking (Eds.), *Blueprints for thinking* (pp. 1-38). New York: Cambridge University Press.

———— (1993). Planning in context: Developmental and situational considerations. *International Journal of Behavioral Development, 16,* 145-167.

Sen, J., & Das, J. P. (1991). Planning competence and managerial excellence: A research framework. In R. F. Mulcahy, R. H. Short, & J. Andrews (Eds.), *Enhancing learning and thinking* (pp. 209-225). New York: Praeger.

Shallice, T. (1988). *From neuropsychology to mental structure.* Cambridge: Cambridge University Press.

Shannon, C. (1948). A mathematical theory of communication. *Bell System Technical Journal, 27,* 379-423.

Shif, Z. I. (1969). Development of children in schools for the mentally retarded. In M. Cole, & I. Maltzman (Eds.), *Handbook of contemporary Soviet psychology* (pp. 326-353). New York: Basic Books.

Shiffrin, R. M., & Schneider, W. (1977). Controlled and automatic human information processing: II. Perceptual learning, automatic attending, and a general theory. *Psychological Review, 84,* 127-190.

Siegler, R. S. (1994). Cognitive variability: A key to understanding cognitive development. *Current Directions in Psychological Science, 3,* 1-5.

Simon, H. A. (1990). Invariants and human behavior. *Annual Review of Psychology, 41,* 1-19.

———— (1992). What is an "explanation" of behavior? *Psychological Science, 3,* 150-161.

Simpson, P. J. (1972). High speed scanning: Stability and generality. *Journal of Experimental Psychology, 96,* 239-246.

Sokolov, A. N. (1969). Studies of speech mechanisms of thinking. In M. Cole & I. Maltzman (Eds.), *Handbook of contemporary Soviet psychology* (pp. 531-573). New York: Basic Books.

———— (1972). *Inner speech and thought.* New York: Plenum Press.

Sophian, C., & Wellman, H. M. (1987). The development of indirect search strategies. *British Journal of Developmental Psychology, 5,* 9-18.

Sperry, R. W. (1993). The impact and promise of the cognitive revolution. *American Psychologist, 48,* 878-885.

Spitz, H. H., & Borys, S. V. (1984). Depth of search: How far can the retarded search through an internally represented problem space? In P. H. Brooks, R. Sperber, & C. McCauley (Eds.), *Learning and cognition in the mentally retarded* (pp. 333-358). Hillsdale, NJ: Erlbaum.

Squire, L. R., Knowlton, B., & Musen, G. (1993). The structure and organization of memory. *Annual Review of Psychology, 44,* 453-495.

Sternberg, S. (1966). High speed scanning in human memory. *Science, 153,* 652-654.

Stuss, D. T. (1992). Biological and psychological development of executive functions. *Brain and Cognition, 20,* 8-23.

Stuss, D. T., & Benson, D. F. (1984). Neuropsychological studies of frontal lobes. *Psychological Bulletin, 95,* 3-28.

———— (1986). *The frontal lobes.* New York: Raven Press.

———— (1987). The frontal lobes and control of cognition and memory. In E. Perecman (Ed.), *Frontal lobes revisited* (pp. 141-158). New York: IRBN Press.

Swanson, J. M., & Briggs, G. E. (1969). Information processing as a function of speed versus accuracy. *Journal of Experimental Psychology, 81,* 223-229.

Tanon, F. (1991). The influences of formal versus informal education on planning skills: A cultural perspective. In J. D. Sinnott, & J. C. Cavanaugh (Eds.), *Bridging paradigms* (pp. 221-235). New York: Praeger.

Teuber, H. L. (1964). The riddle of frontal lobe function in man. In J. M. Warren & K. Akert (Eds.), *The frontal granular cortex and behavior* (pp. 410-444). New York: McGraw-Hill.

Teuber, H. L., Battersby, W. S., & **Bender, M. B.** (1949). Changes in visual searching performance following cerebral lesions. *The American Journal of Physiology, 159,* 592.

———— (1951). Performance of complex visual tasks after cerebral lesions. *Journal of Nervous and Mental Diseases, 114,* 413-429.

Thatcher, R. W. (1991). Maturation of human frontal lobes: Physiological evidence for staging. *Developmental Neuropsychology, 7,* 397-419.

———— (1992). Cyclic cortical reorganization during early childhood. *Brain and Cognition, 20,* 24-50.

Thatcher, R. W., Walker, R. A., & **Giudice, S.** (1987). Human cerebral hemispheres develop at different rate and ages. *Science, 236,* 1110-1113.

Thelen, E. (1992). Development as a dynamic system. *Current Directions in Psychological Science, 1,* 189-193.

Thorpe, W. H. (1956). *Learning and instinct in animals.* Cambridge, MA: Harvard University Press.

Tinbergen, N. (1951). *The study of instinct.* Oxford: Oxford University Press.

Tolman, E. C. (1948). Cognitive maps in rats and men. *Psychological Review, 55,* 189-208.

Treisman, A. (1982). Perceptual grouping and attention in visual search for features and for objects. *Journal of Experimental Psychology: Human Perception and Performance, 8,* 194-214.

Treisman, A., & **Gelade, S.** (1980). A feature integration theory of attention. *Cognitive Psychology, 12,* 97-136.

Treisman, A., & **Gormican, S.** (1988). Feature analysis in early vision: Evidence from search asymmetries. *Psychological Review, 95,* 15-48.

Tudge, J. (1989). When collaboration leads to regression: Some negative consequences of socio-cognitive conflict. *European Journal of Social Psychology, 19,* 123-138.

Van der Veer, R., & **van I Jzendoorn, M. H.** (1988). Early childhood attachment and later problem solving: A Vygotskian perspective. In J. Valsiner (Ed.), *Child development within culturally structured environments. Vol. 1: Parental cognition and adult-child interaction* (pp. 215-246). Norwood, NJ: Ablex.

Vygotsky, L. S. (1962). *Thought and language.* Edited and translated by E. Hanfmann & G. Vakar. Cambridge, MA: The MIT Press.

———— (1978). *Mind in society.* Edited and translated by M. Cole, V. John-Steiner, S. Scribner, & E. Souberman. Cambridge, MA: Harvard University Press.

———— (1986). *Thought and language.* Edited and translated by A. Kozulin. Cambridge, MA: The MIT Press.

Wellman, H. M., Fabricius, W. V., & **Sophian, C.** (1985). The early development of planning. In H. M. Wellman (Ed.), *Children's searching* (pp. 123-149). Hillsdale, NJ: Erlbaum.

Wellman, H. M., Somerville, S. C., Revelle, G. L., Haake, R. J., & **Sophian, C.** (1984). The development of comprehensive search skills. *Child Development, 55,* 471-481.

Welsh, M. C., & **Pennington, B. F.** (1988). Assessing frontal lobe functioning in children: Views from developmental psychology. *Developmental Neuropsychology, 4,* 199-230.

Welsh, M. C., Pennington, B. F., & **Groisser, D. B.** (1991). A normative-developmental study of executive function. *Developmental Neuropsychology, 7,* 131-149.

Wertsch, J. V. (1982). Introduction. In A. R. Luria, *Language and cognition.* New York: John Wiley & Sons.

————— (1991). *Voices of the mind.* Cambridge, MA: Harvard University Press.

Wickens, C. D. (1984). Processing resources in attention. In R. Parasuraman & R. Davies (Eds.), *Varieties of attention* (pp. 63-102). New York: Academic Press.

Willatts, P. (1984). The stage-IV infant's solution of problems requiring the use of supports. *Infant Behaviour and Development, 7,* 125-134.

Zimmer, H. (1951). *Philosophies of India.* London: Routledge & Kegan Paul.